FIREBRANDS

PORTRAITS FROM THE AMERICAS

FIREBRANDS

PORTRAITS FROM THE AMERICAS

Justseeds Artists' Cooperative

Edited by Shaun Slifer and Bec Young

Firebrands: Portraits from the Americas
Justseeds Artists' Cooperative
www.justseeds.org
Edited by Shaun Slifer and Bec Young
Cover illustration by Pete Yahnke

First Edition of 5,000 copies
2010

This is Microcosm #76079
ISBN 978-1-934620-68-7

Microcosm Publishing
222 S Rogers St.
Bloomington, IN 47404
www.microcosmpublishing.com

We have other books, zines, t-shirts, patches, stickers, videos, and things available from our catalog.

Distributed by AK Press, Oakland, California
(510) 208-1700 /sales@akpress.org
Available through Baker & Taylor, Ingram, and finer bookstores.

{CONTENTS}

THIS BOOK IS FOR anyone who has sat, trembling with frustration and disappointment, in a history class that was neither stimulating nor inclusive. It's for those tired of hauling to classes heavy textbooks that have been carefully edited to remove anything interesting or useful. It's for all our ancestors, especially those misrepresented in those schoolbooks, left out because they were too brown, too female, too poor, too queer, too uneducated, too disabled, or because they daydreamed too much. It's for all those who, right now, are working to create the world that they want to live in.

Firebrands is a short primer on people we admire for their tenacity and courage, people who fought for their dreams of freedom and equality and some who fight still. We hope that in these introductions, their stories will light a spark. We want you to stick this book in your back pocket, and stick these stories in your mind. We realize that like all humans, our admired characters collected here come with a fair amount of contradiction, and their stories can't be separated from the time and conditions in which they lived. It may not be possible to look at the past objectively, without the prejudices of our own time, but passing on the knowledge of where we have been is perhaps the only honest way to illuminate where to go from here.

We edited this book carefully, with an emphasis on factual accuracy as we located information. It's not meant to present the "most important" or "most influential" people, but rather a collection of inspirations. And while we chose to limit our scope to the Americas, in hopes of challenging an ethnocentric view of what "America" is made of, it is clear that the same centrism made it difficult for us to know or find the stories that could be culled from beyond U.S. borders. Misinformation, repression and the lack of conclusive records about innumerable fascinating figures remains a problem in navigating our radical histories. While we tried to be inclusive, this series of portraits is just a point from which to start. With the resources section in the back of this book, we intend to lead you toward deeper learning and action.

The 78 people profiled in this book were compiled by 20 illustrators, who also contributed preliminary research and, in some cases, wrote the accompanying profiles. The layout and design were the efforts of Bec Young, with Pete Yahnke illustrating the cover and Colin Matthes contributing page titles. Shaun Slifer did much of the research and writing, with generous editing help from Jessie Gray Singer and Bec Young. Josh MacPhee contributed his expert advice and keen eye, and Molly Fair used her secret librarian resources and contributed to the index.

In particular, this book is gratefully dedicated to Howard Zinn, who did so much to promote a people's version of history, and who passed away while we were in the final stages of preparing this book for print.

This is for the storytellers, and for those of us whose hunger for stories goes beyond that which we have been fed.

Bec Young and Shaun Slifer
2010

Shaun would like to extend special thanks to Bob Helms, Julie Herrada, Ross Winn, Dennis Moody, and Dr. Timothy Sutherlund.

"Beto [age 10] sends a message with his uncle so that among the demands of the EZLN there be one about raising the ocean to the sky and lowering the sky to the ocean... Beto thinks the change will not be too complicated.
They're both blue, right? Both big? Anyway, Nabor [age 3] says it's simpler to change the world than for us to learn how to walk on our heads. For Beto and Nabor happiness would be stooping in order to see the sky."
~Subcomandante Marcos,
Zapatista Army of National Liberation,
"Dignity Cannot be Studied, You Either Live it or it Dies."

SOMEONE SHOULD HAVE TOLD you already.

By the time you're old enough to start asking *why?*, older people should start helping you understand why the world is the way it is, and what has been done to change it. That's what "history" means. History is about the choices that human beings have made and keep making, about how they want to live and why they want to live.

If you don't learn history, and I mean learn it like the way you learn to love music, poetry and kissing, then the world will always be a mystery to you, and you'll have to stumble through your days without being able to make any sense of what's happening, or what you could possibly do differently. History is necessary, you need it to live a good life. But unlike food, or water, or even love, you *can* actually live your whole life thinking that understanding history is completely pointless. In fact, many people do feel that way, even many of the people who make careers of teaching children history in school. They teach history like it's just a bunch of facts to memorize, just a time-line between "a long time ago" and "now." They don't think anything can be done to change society for the better, and so they themselves do nothing to stand against injustice. These kind of teachers do worse than nothing, because they teach children to accept, to keep quiet, to follow orders.

So, someone should have told you these stories already, but they probably didn't. That's not your fault. Rebels, radicals, bank robbers, and runaway slaves have never been given too much space in history books. The slave-traders, bankers, and war-makers have been flattering themselves with the lie that they are the "Great Men" of history, but meanwhile there have been thousands and millions more of us who have thrown ourselves into the tremendously hard and beautiful project of being free. This book is the story of just 78 of those people.

Here you will read the stories of people who lived incredible lives; lives that were much more full, much more *alive* than most people's. They tried harder. They took more risks. They were less afraid. They put overwhelming value in joy and love. They felt pulled to try to end the suffering of fellow human beings. They refused to just "get by" and demanded to dream of new and more beautiful ways of life. It's for these reasons—and not wealth, power, or status—that people should be honored and admired.

Okay, but this is important. These great people also made quite a bit of trouble, and often paid a serious price for their ideas, their values, and their actions. We should never forget that many of these people were either ridiculed, hated, jailed, or at war, or on the run, or executed... or all of the above.

You should ask yourself, under what circumstances would you take these kinds of risks? What is worth so much to you that you're willing to fight for it, willing to risk losing your job, your home, your family... even your life? Chief Sitting Bull's teachings encouraged a group of warriors of the Lakota nation to fight against the U.S. military as if they were "bullet-proof." Zumbi's community of runaway slaves in Brazil taught themselves the martial art Capoeira in order to fight off anyone who might try and take them back to slavery. Emma Goldman's partner Alexander Berkman was so sure that capitalism is an inhumane system that he shot a factory owner in the face and went to jail. Emma agreed with Berkman so strongly that she helped to dig a tunnel under the fence of the prison to set him free. Fifty years later, close friends of Assata Shakur, from the Black Liberation Army, helped Assata break out of jail and escape to Cuba.

Refusing to go along with a system that treats you and others like trash doesn't always mean you have to be an outlaw or go to war. We're not all facing life in prison, or slavery, or genocide. We're in different kinds of messes, depending on where we were born, and what kind of possibilities seem immediately obvious to us. Surely the problems facing a child in a boarding school in Vermont are going to be very different from the problems a street kid in São Paulo has to deal with. But nonetheless— and whether we know it or not—our destinies have been tied together for centuries. Hopefully you can see, bit by bit as you read through this book, that in all the places that we now call home, from Nova Scotia all the way down to Buenos Aires, for as far as back as our grandparents' grandparents can remember, people have been looking for ways to break out of their chains. As C.L.R. James said, "We were not able to choose the mess we were born into—this collapse of a whole society—but we are able to choose our way out."

The simple question then is: what seems so fucked up, so totally unacceptable, that you'd be willing to lose the respect of your friends, family and co-workers because you just can't go along with their way of life?

There are things worth fighting for in this world. There are dreams worth dying for. *People are not born heroes.* All of the people included in this book were born, just like you and me, into a social system which charted out for them what they should expect to do with their lives; and all of them made a different choice. They found themselves up against conditions of life that they simply couldn't tolerate, and they found a way—whether big or small—to stand up against the things that were oppressing them. Living a more full life is a choice, and any of us can make it—at any time.

Now that you've got ahold of these stories, let them sink in deep, underneath your skin and into your bloodstream. These stories are your inheritance, a gift from people who, having never met you, and without being related to you or necessarily able even to speak your language, all the same acted so that you could live more fully, could be more free.

Taylor Sparrow, 2010

FIREBRANDS

NO! I'm not going 10,000 miles from home to help murder and burn another poor nation simply to continue the domination of white slave masters over the darker people the world over. This is the day when such evils must come to an end. I have been warned that to take such a stand would cost me millions of dollars. But I have said it once and I will say it again. The real enemy of my people is here.

— Muhammad Ali

Colin Matthes

Muhammad Ali

FIGHTING HIS WAY INTO the national spotlight during the rise of civil rights struggles in the United States, the brash and outspoken Muhammad Ali made ripples internationally. Simply put, Ali did not act like a popular athlete was supposed to. Born Cassius Clay in working class Louisville, Kentucky, Ali brought home a gold medal from the 1960 Olympics in Rome at age 18. A black man returning with an international victory for the U.S., he was denied service in a Louisville diner, gold medal or not. He threw his award into the Ohio River.

At 22, Ali deftly took the title of heavyweight boxing champion of the world, and on the following day announced that he had joined the Nation of Islam. The incredible media fervor surrounding his Muslim conversion and name change, combined with Ali's friendship with Malcolm X, reiterated the foundational racism of the U.S. to a population already seething for revolutionary change. A powerful and resolute hero to millions of people of color, the boxer was audacious both in the ring and in interviews. The threat of Ali's enormous potential to influence masses of the working class with his opinions and courage terrified the status quo.

In 1966, Muhammad Ali was drafted by the U.S. Army. Although it was clear that the celebrity Ali would not see active combat, he steadfastly refused any military service. Giving up his heavyweight title and millions of dollars, and risking his freedom and career, Ali was banned from boxing for almost four years for following his conscience. Ali's actions resonated around the globe. He was a forceful voice in opposition to the war in Vietnam, a black man with courage and conviction and a fearless dissenter in a world where "jocks" were not supposed to be radically minded.

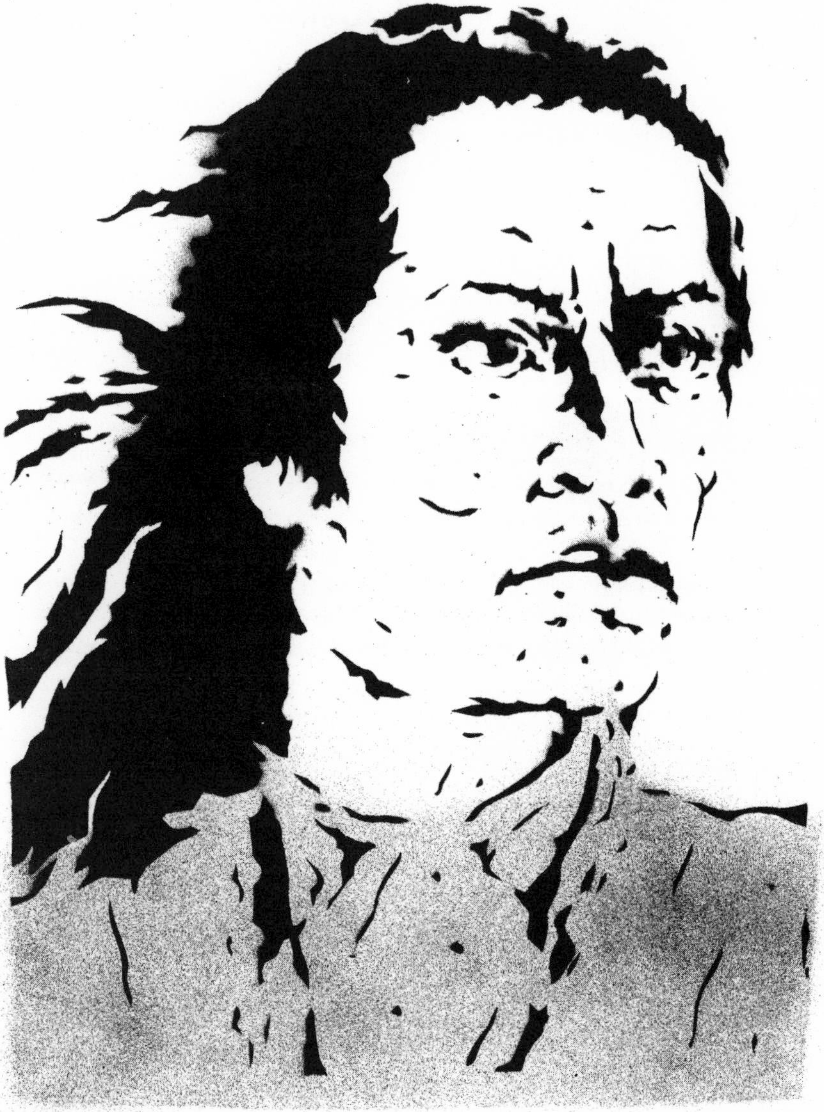

Chris Stain

Túpac Amaru II

JOSÉ GABRIEL CONDORCANQUI NOGUERA was a *mestizo* (person of mixed race) who claimed direct lineage through his father to the last Incan chief, Túpac Amaru. Born in a time when nine-tenths of the populations of the Andean region were still enslaved and indebted to the Spanish colonists, the man who would later take the name Túpac Amaru II would become a legendary symbol of struggle for generations to come.

Tired of consistently petitioning for better working conditions for his people, Amaru boldly organized an armed revolution in Peru in 1780. He planned and carried out the kidnapping and public execution of a Cuzco governor, Antonio de Arriaga. The killing sparked a full-scale rebellion of thousands of Peruvian workers, who rallied behind Amaru and fought several battles against Spanish soldiers and native loyalists. While Amaru's forces occupied many provinces, he soon found that he could not control the rage and indignation of his volunteer army. Fueled by decades of violent oppression, his soldiers slaughtered anyone they saw as an oppressor, yet this made it politically difficult for Amaru to gain outside support for his insurrection. Betrayed by two of his own officers after failing to take Cuzco, Amaru was brutalized by his Spanish captors, who tried unsuccessfully to quarter him with horses before beheading him. Although the rebellion was stopped, it was the first large-scale revolution in the region in 200 years, and provided a renewed source of inspiration for future struggles against slavery and oppression.

"When I write it feels like I'm carving bone. It feels like Im creating my own face, my own heart-a Nahuatl concept. My soul makes itself through the creative act. It is constantly remaking and giving birth to itself through the creative act."

Melanie Cervantes

Gloria Anzaldúa

{SEPTEMBER 26, 1942 - MAY 15, 2004}

ONE OF THE FIRST openly lesbian Chicana writers in the U.S., Gloria Anzaldúa was born in south Texas to migrant farmer parents. Anzaldúa was a poet, social theorist, and writer of children's books. Her work has had a poignant impact on postcolonial feminist theory. While keeping an open mind to the experience of the individual, she consistently challenged people to recognize and transform their own racism, homophobia, and unintentional ignorance.

Many of Anzaldúas' works weave the English, Spanish, and Nahuatl languages together, most significantly her book *Borderlands*, published in 1987. Anzaldúa described this work as *autohistoria-teoría*, a genre that encompassed the life-story while transforming normative Western autobiographical forms. Her method of shifting between multiple languages in her writing illustrated her theories of a *mestizaje* (mixed race) or threshold identity, people who could walk cultural margins and thus directly challenge binary categories in the Western world. She also coined the term *nepantlera,* a unique and visionary people who could move through various social stratifications and identities in order to bring positive change to more people. Always deeply spiritual, it was crucial to Anzaldúa that people understand and incorporate both the conflicting and consistent identities within themselves, to gain new perspectives and challenge the oppressive cultural norms in their lives.

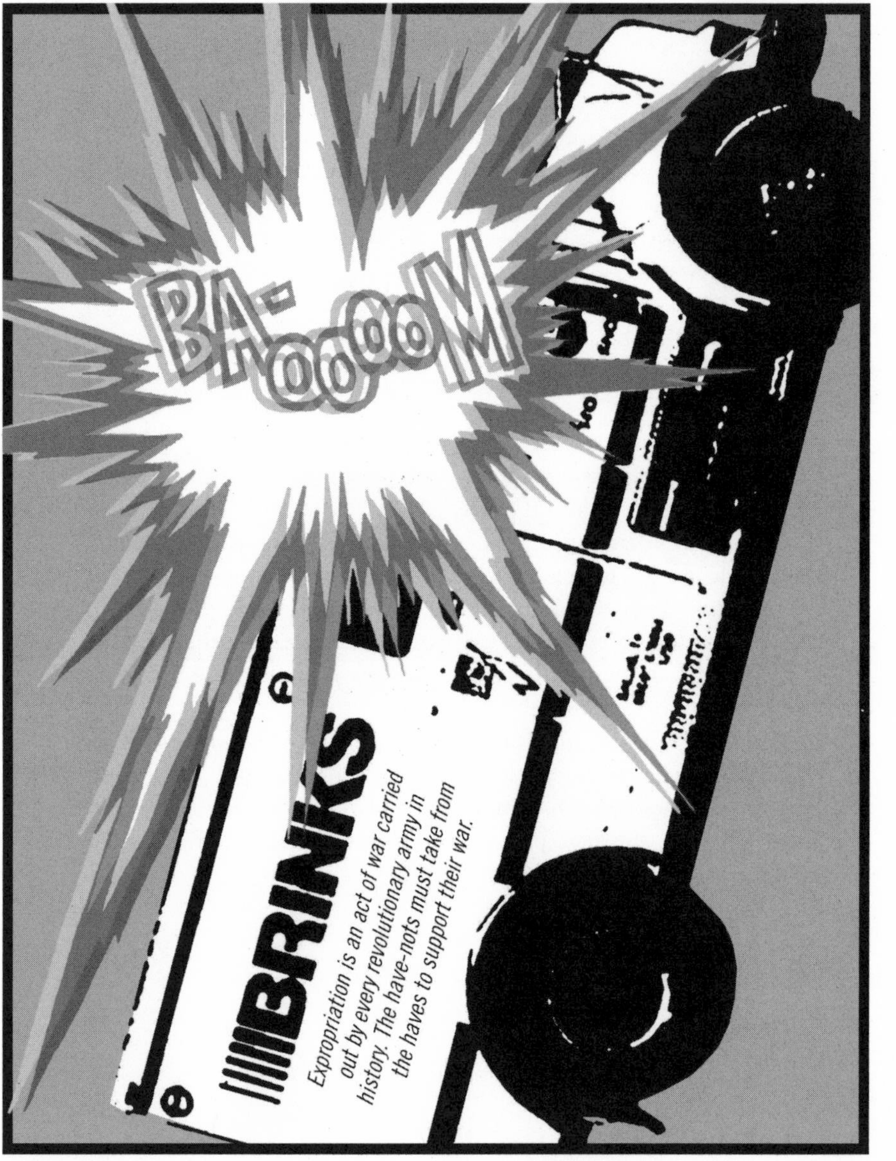
BA-OOOOM
BRINKS
Expropriation is an act of war carried out by every revolutionary army in history. The have-nots must take from the haves to support their war.

Kuwasi Balagoon

{December 22, 1946 - December 13, 1986}

KUWASI BALAGOON STRUGGLED FOR the majority of his life against racism, U.S. colonialism, and capitalist exploitation. In his early twenties, while in the U.S. Army, he and other black soldiers formed a clandestine group called De Legislators, which attacked and beat racist white soldiers. Upon his return to civilian life he joined the Black Panther Party. He was one of the defendants in the Panther 21 case tried in New York City, in which the State of New York claimed that the Black Panthers were planning to bomb multiple locations in the city. Balagoon and the rest of the Panthers were acquitted of all charges.

As the 1960s turned to the 70s, the Black Panthers collapsed under the weight of state repression and infighting. Balagoon and a number of other New York Panthers went underground, and became a part of the Black Liberation Army (BLA), a decentralized guerrilla force fighting to liberate black people in the U.S. Balagoon and many others in the BLA believed that in order to overthrow racism and capitalism, they needed to build the Republic of New Africa (RNA), a separate black nation that would be carved out of the southeastern United States. Interestingly, he also became an avowed anarchist, trying to balance his belief in decentralization and autonomy (seen in the organization of the BLA), with the more top-down and traditional nation-state political model of the RNA. Balagoon was sentenced to prison multiple times for his underground activities in the 1970s, and each time he escaped and returned to his clandestine life as a BLA soldier. In 1982, he was caught and charged with murder for his participation in a Brinks armored truck robbery. He was convicted and sentenced to 75 years to life, but died in December 1986 from AIDS-related complications. Resistant to the end, Balagoon had been an anarchist amongst nationalists and communists, and a bisexual man within a sexually conservative black liberation movement.

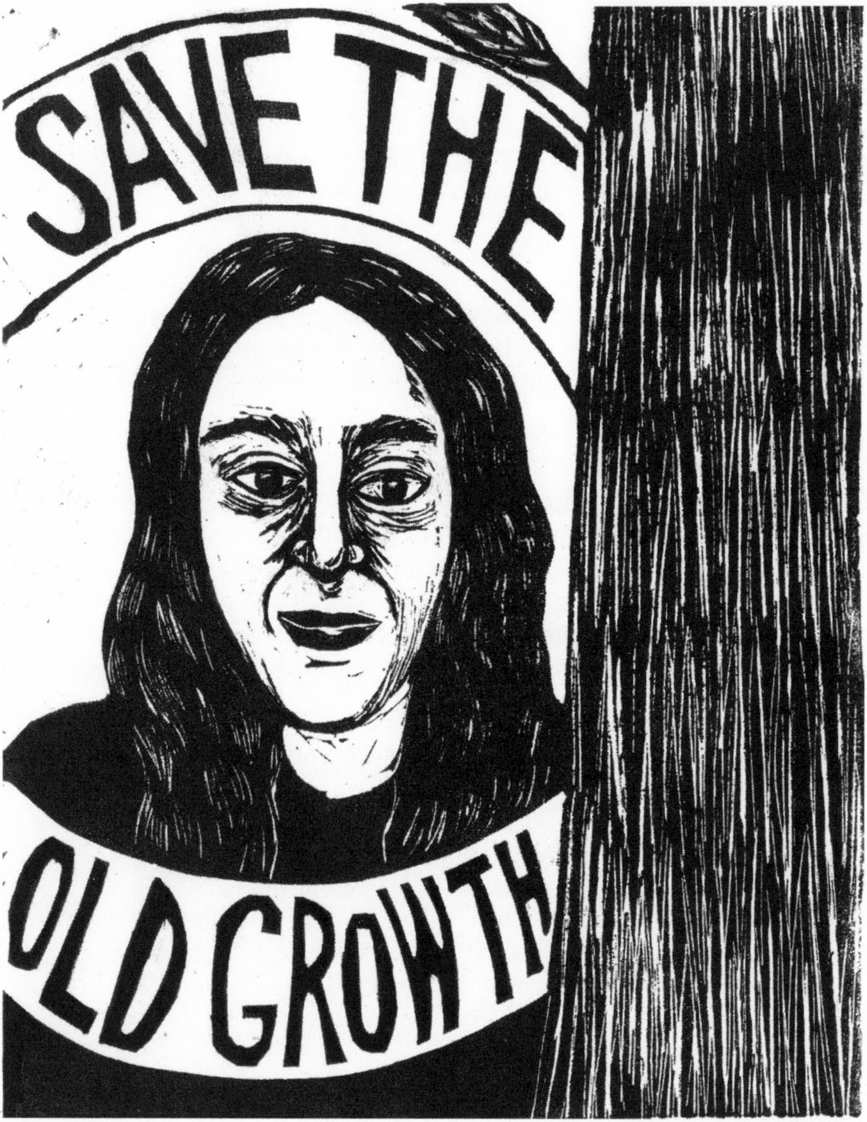
SAVE THE
OLD GROWTH

Meredith Stern

Judi Bari

"We need to build a society that is not based on the exploitation of the Earth at all—a society whose goal is to achieve a stable state with nature for the benefit of all species."

JUDI BARI IS BEST remembered for her work against the unsustainable liquidation logging of the lush forests of the Pacific Northwest. She found her passion and direction while working a carpentry job that was installing 1,000-year-old forest timber in the interior of an upscale luxury residence. Putting to use the experience she gained as a union organizer and anti-war activist during the Vietnam War, Bari worked tenaciously for the preservation of old-growth forests, while dismantling the common gender barriers of activism. Working with Darryl Cherney and joining in the efforts of Earth First!, Bari helped draw attention to timber issues through nonviolent direct action, and succeeded in rallying thousands to the cause and drawing nationwide attention to her bioregion.

Judi Bari understood the interconnectedness of the issues for which she was campaigning, particularly the fundamental notion that rural people, both timber workers and residents, were at the heart of the environmental struggle. With the IWW, she took positive steps to build an alliance between timber workers and environmental activists, and for her efforts the FBI took a keen interest in Bari and her peers. A determined timber industry smear campaign saw Bari and others receiving anonymous threats on their lives. On May 4, 1990, while driving with Cherney on a campaign tour, a pipe bomb exploded under the driver's seat in her car. The FBI accused the two activists of having made the device and placed them under arrest, sparking a massive media frenzy that reverberates with misinformation today. Although Bari lost a battle with breast cancer in 1997, Cherney and her family and friends won a civil suit in 2002 claiming that the two had been targeted and wrongly arrested in order to silence their activism.

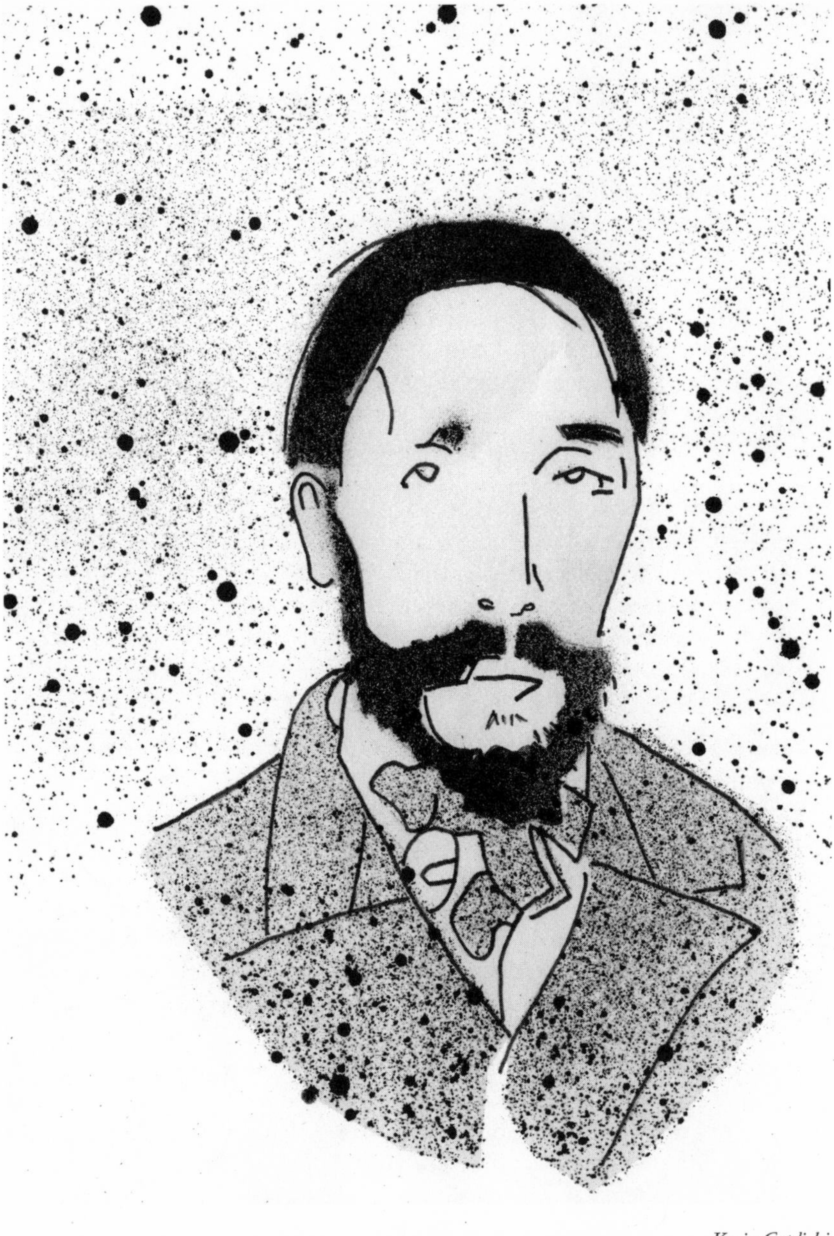

Kevin Caplicki

Rafael Barrett

"The laws and constitutions that govern peoples by force are phony. They are not the products of men's inquiry and common advancement. They are the creatures of a barbarous minority that resorts to brute force in order to indulge its avarice and cruelty."

LITTLE IS WRITTEN ABOUT the revolutionary writer Rafael Barrett that has been translated into English. Although he was born in Spain and died in France, it was his brief seven years in South America, five of those in Paraguay, where Barrett left his resounding mark. An avowed anarchist, Barrett was a prolific writer who left a brief but fiery trail of philosophical accusations against the rule of law, all while working day jobs as a science teacher or for the government's engineering agency in Asuncion. His well-circulated writings upheld the equality of women and proclaimed that family, not any government, should be at the core of a truly just society.

His editorial journalism is perhaps his most well-known work, and also that which brought to Barrett the most troubles with authorities. The essay *Lo Que Son los Yerbales (What the Maté Plantations Are)* was a cannon blast leveled at the yerba maté tea industry and the appalling, but not widely understood, conditions for maté laborers. The essay, influenced by Barrett's larger critique of global imperialist economies, dissected the deceptive recruitment policies and systematic worker indebtedness upheld by the maté companies; policies that resulted in the virtual slavery of plantation workers under working conditions that echoed the coal mines of the United States. Even Barrett's journalistic forays would bear the distinct and expressively angry voice common in his polemic criticisms of higher powers; for this he was forced into exile in Brazil and later Uruguay. Barrett succumbed to tuberculosis at the age of 34 while seeking medical treatment in France, unemployable due to his ill health but continuing to write and publish until his last days.

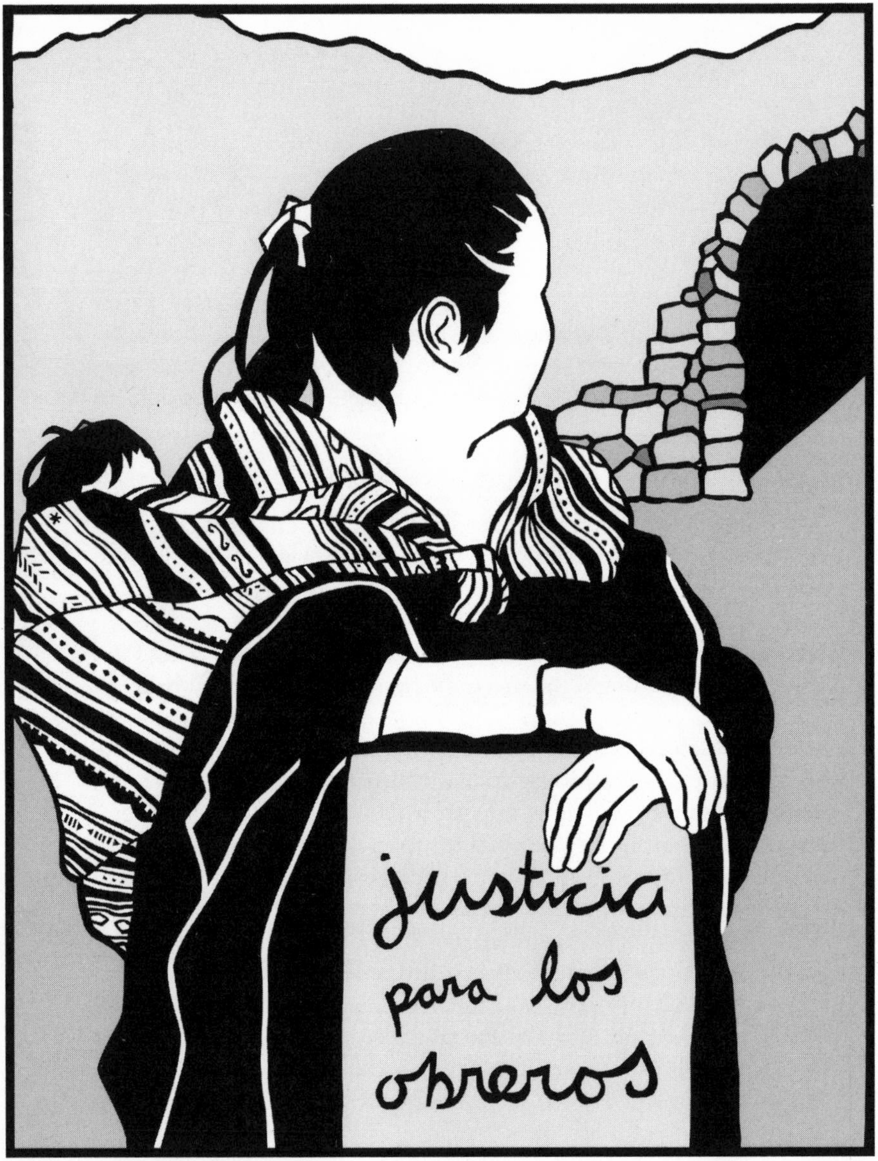
justicia
para los
obreros

Kristine Virsis

Domitila Barrios de Chungara

"I want to leave future generations the only valid inheritance: a free country and social justice."

DOMITILA BARRIOS DE CHUNGARA was born in 1937 in the tin-mining districts of Siglo XX, Bolivia. After her father was blacklisted for organizing mine workers to unionize, her family moved to Pulacayo where they endured extreme poverty. At the age of 10, Chungara's mother died. Her father succumbed to alcoholism and became physically abusive, leaving her to care for her four younger sisters and their home. She struggled to stay in school in a time when it was considered unnecessary for girls to be literate or formally educated.

In the early 1960s, Chungara was instrumental in the creation and administration of the Housewives Committee in Siglo XX, which put pressure on the government to improve living conditions for miners and their families. For her organizational efforts, she was imprisoned, tortured, and eventually exiled from her hometown. Despite her treatment by the Bolivian government, Chungara went on to become an internationally recognized voice for indigenous miners' and women's rights. In 1977, the 23-day hunger strike she organized with four other women drew massive attention, and is credited with helping topple the military regime of Hugo Banzer. Chungara argues that women need to be full participants in social and economic justice movements, educating themselves to overcome the socialization that has taught them to defer to men. She believes that the liberation of women is fundamentally linked to the socioeconomic, political and cultural liberation of all. Domatilia Barrios de Chungara continues to live in Bolivia, where she founded the Domitila Mobile School in 1990.

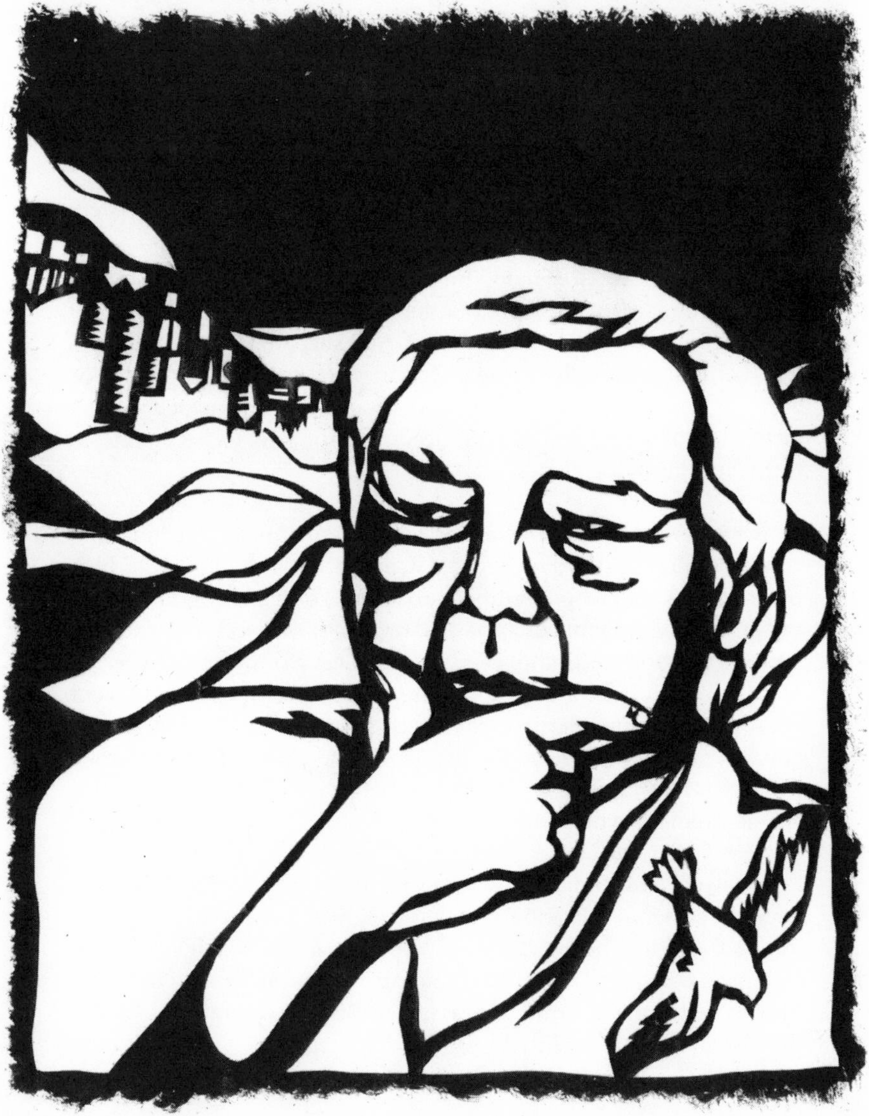

Bec Young

"We are the leaders we've been looking for."

GRACE LEE BOGGS (born Chin Yuk Ping or Jade Peace Chin) is an activist and intellectual whose visionary thinking has been crucial to social transformation movements, particularly in the post-industrial Rust Belt cities of the United States. Grace grew up in New York City, where her father, who managed to immigrate to the U.S. in the early 1900s despite the Chinese Exclusion Act of 1882, owned a restaurant. After earning a Ph.D in philosophy from Bryn Mawr College in 1940, Grace was intellectually engaged for almost 20 years in the Marxist group the Johnson-Forest Tendency, along with C.L.R. James and Raya Dunayevskaya.

In 1953, Grace travelled to Detroit, Michigan, where she met and eventually married James "Jimmy" Boggs, an African-American labor activist and writer from southern Alabama who had made his way to Detroit to find work in the Chrysler auto plant. The two worked together as partners in revolution until Jimmy's death in 1993. They founded organizations and movements, fostered dialogues and events, and wrote books and essays. During those years, Detroit changed dramatically from a center of industrial power to a city desperately lacking in resources and population due to automation in the factories, deindustrialization as well as institutional and personal racism.

The Boggs' work focused on justice for African-Americans, expanding the basic concepts of the civil rights movement to include thoughtful and nuanced ideas about class-consciousness. They promoted the ideal of "active citizenship", in which people are empowered of their own accord to make positive changes in their neighborhood, city or country. Among the movements co-founded by Grace was Detroit Summer, a "multicultural, intergenerational youth program to rebuild, redefine, re-spirit Detroit from the ground up."

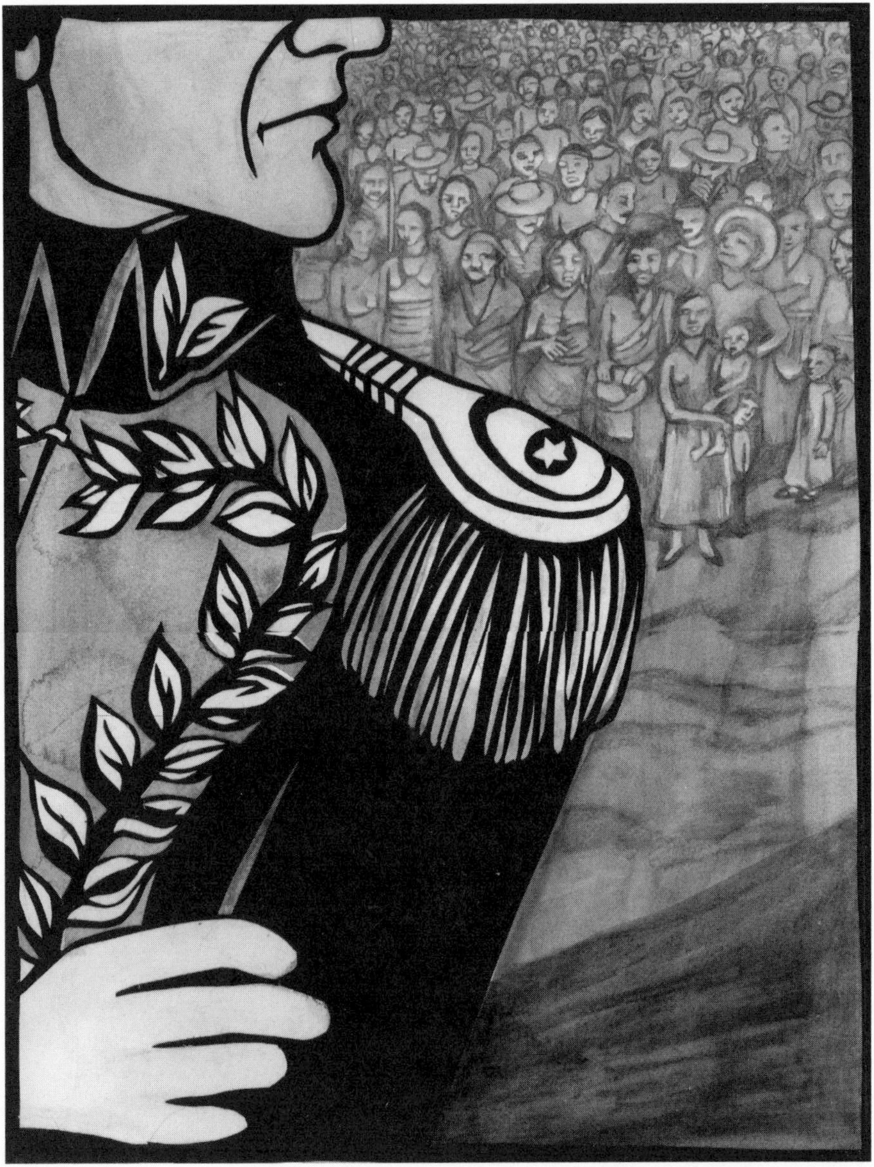

Bec Young

"Judgement comes from experience, and experience comes from bad judgement."

LEGENDARY IN THE HISTORY of the struggle for Latin American independence, Simón Bolívar was the military leader and visionary credited with the liberation of six countries from colonial rule: Bolivia, Ecuador, Peru, Colombia, Venezuela, and Panama (formerly part of Colombia). Bolívar was born into a long bloodline of wealth and comfort in what is now Venezuela, and was educated in Spain and France as a young man. He returned to his homeland in 1807 to participate in the insurrectionary juntas that sprang up as the Spanish colonies began to boil over with unrest. Only 30 years prior, the United States was born out of struggle against the British. In 1789, the French Revolution reverberated across the Atlantic, and the former slave turned general, Toussaint L'Ouverture, would lead an insurrection for the independence of Haiti (then Saint-Domingue) soon after. Spanish influence in Europe was crumbling, and Simón Bolívar and others began the bloody work of overthrowing the last of Spanish rule in their homelands.

Bolívar financed much of his revolution with the funds he inherited, money made from copper mines and slave labor. However, unlike his counterpart revolutionary leaders in the burgeoning United States, Bolívar was anti-slavery from the beginning and always concerned with addressing the violent plight of Indigenous people who had been fighting to maintain their cultures since Columbus arrived three centuries earlier. His vision was for a unified South, a federation of independent republics and a central government tasked only with upholding the rights of the individual. Far from realizing that dream in his lifetime, Simón Bolívar is nevertheless celebrated as a hero throughout Latin America.

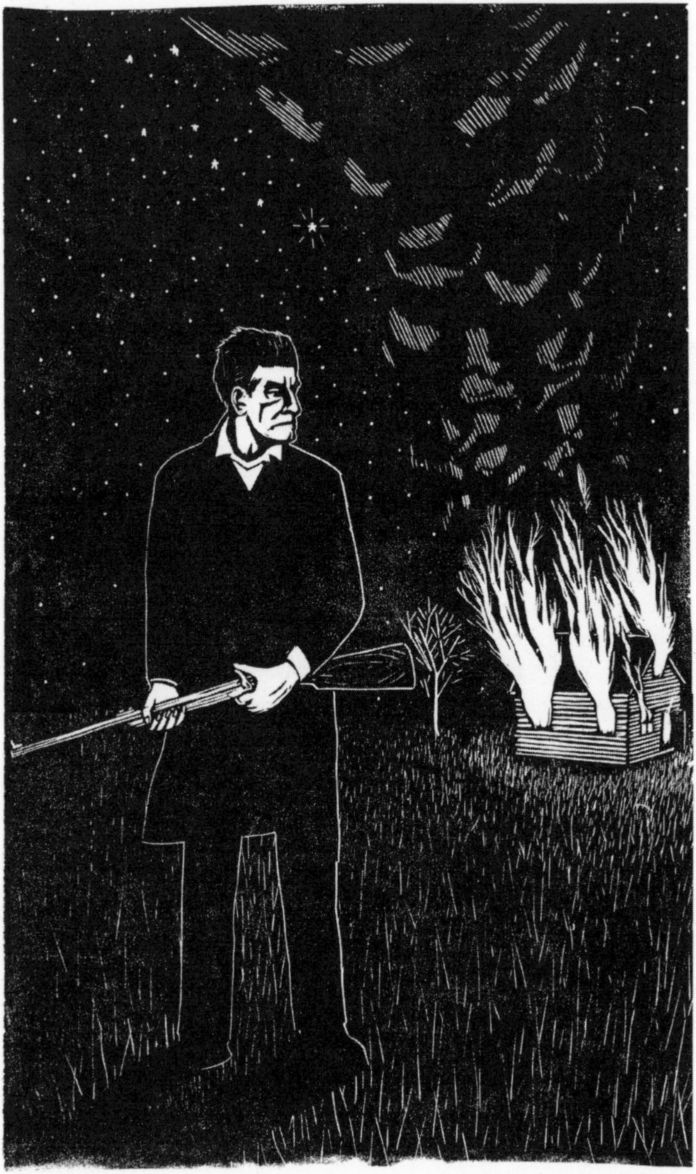

Alec "Icky" Dunn

"I, John Brown, am now quite certain that the crimes of this guilty land will never be purged away but with blood."

FEW PEOPLE WHOSE DEEDS are taught in public school history textbooks are as loaded with controversy as those of John Brown. A militant abolitionist and Christian who advocated for—and practiced—violent opposition to slavery, often Brown's life is either celebrated as that of a visionary hero and martyr or decried as that of an ideologically corrupt terrorist.

Born into a deeply religious Connecticut family, Brown couldn't complete the necessary schooling to become a minister due to financial constraints. As an agricultural entrepreneur, Brown came into contact with many abolitionists, and was drawn to the cause of freedom for slaves through both his personal and religious convictions. Learning of the campaign of violence wrought by pro-slavery forces in the burgeoning state of Kansas, he began to believe that fire could only be fought with fire, and moved to the Midwest to engage in guerilla combat.

John Brown's legacy is typically whittled down to his audacious orchestration of an armed slave revolt in Harper's Ferry, West Virginia, which failed. Brown campaigned tirelessly for funds, munitions and soldiers to lead an armed insurrection of thousands. However, his October, 1859 raid on an armory saw Brown with only 21 armed supporters, all of whom were eventually overcome by a force of U.S. Marines, led by General Robert E. Lee. Brown was hung that winter for murder, conspiracy and treason. The American Civil War, commonly characterized as a battle over the issue of slavery, would tear apart the U.S. a year and a half later.

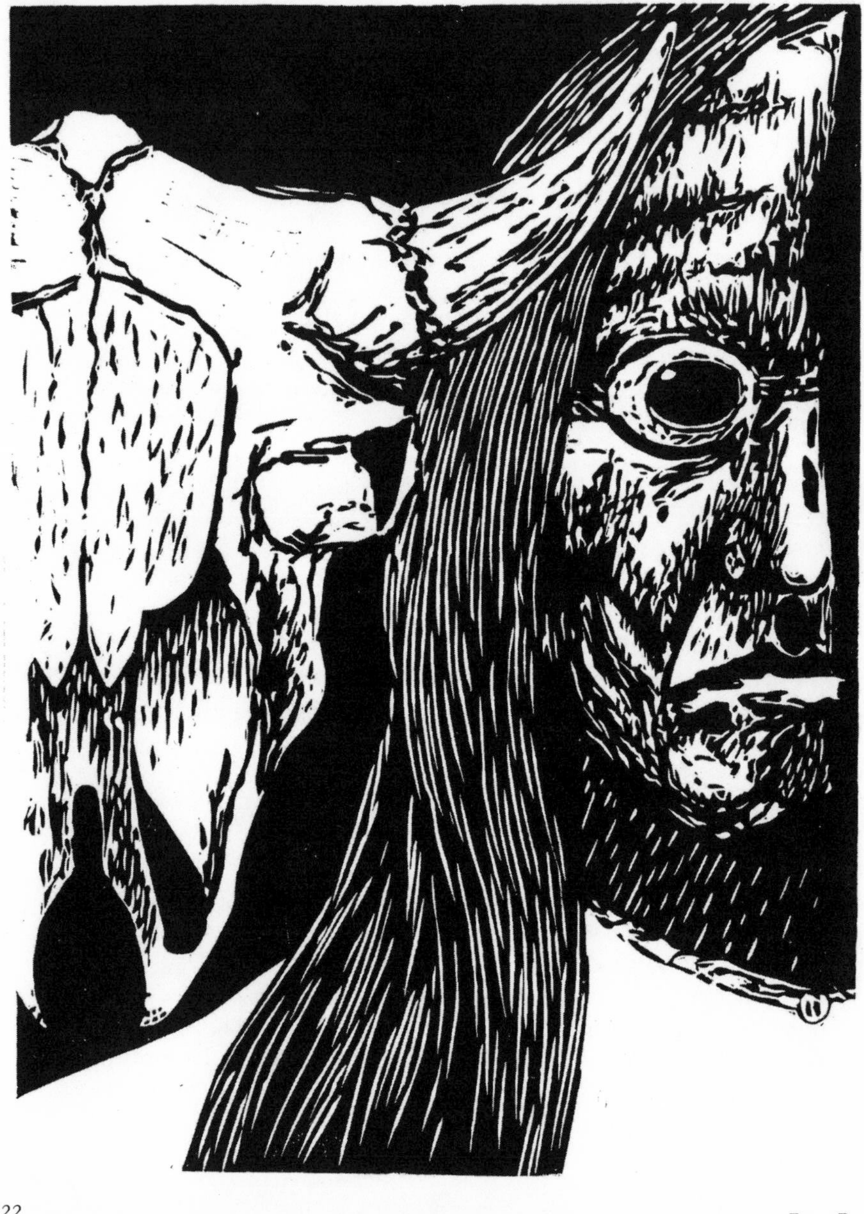

Roger Peet

Sitting Bull

"A warrior/ I have been/ now/ it is all over/ a hard time/ I have"

KNOWN AS SITTING BULL, Tȟatȟáŋka Íyotake was a chief of the Hunkpapa Lakota Sioux and a leader during a time of cultural and ecological annihilation. As settlers pressed westward, the First Nations of the Great Plains watched in horror as their lands were laid to waste. Settlers forced natives from their hunting grounds, blocked their migration routes and began a slaughter of the great Buffalo herds that drove the beasts to the brink of extinction. The natives resisted, skirmishing with settlers and on occasion scoring significant military victories. Most notable among these was the triumph at the Little Bighorn River, where massed Sioux warriors obliterated a force of U.S. troops led by George Armstrong Custer. Sitting Bull led the Sioux in that battle and many others, but all the bravery of the Plains tribes was never enough to turn back the deluge of settler immigrants and their lust for land, gold and dominion.

Long years of struggle and defeat stretched ahead. Sitting Bull spent later years of his life performing in Buffalo Bill's Wild West Show, a touring display of heavily stereotyped frontier culture and folklore. Near his life's end, he became a disciple of the prophet Wovoka, whose Ghost Dance religion prophesied the imminent destruction of settler society. The Plains tribes had been decimated by disease and war and had been herded onto tiny reservations that represented the poorest corners of their ancestral territories. The Ghost Dancers believed that the plains would soon be washed clean of the untrustworthy whites, that the streams would run clear and game once more would be plentiful. Sitting Bull's allegiance to the Ghost Dance increased the fear that he inspired in the settlers. Eventually, Sitting Bull was killed by Indian police at his cabin in the lonesome prison that the reservations had become.

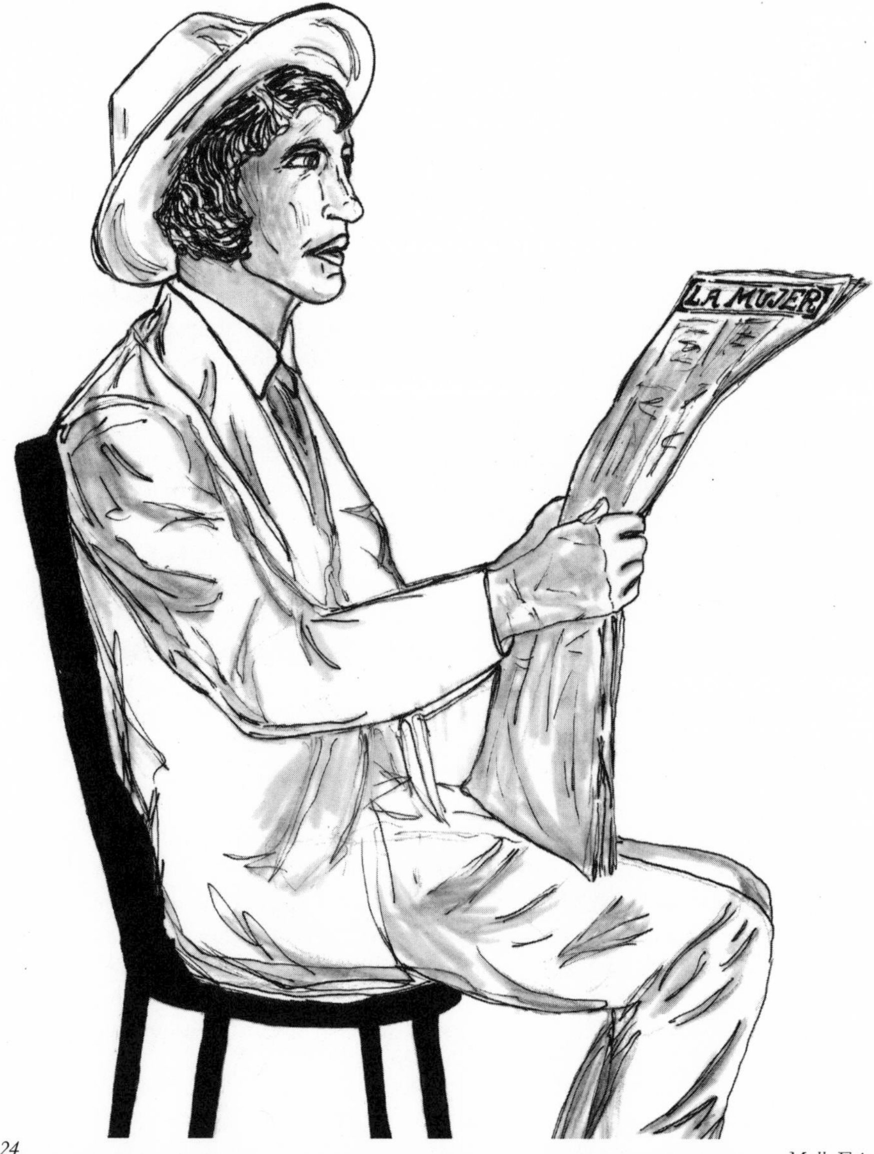
LA MUJER

Molly Fair

Luisa Capetillo

"Tyranny, like freedom, has no country, any more than do exploiters or workers."

LUISA CAPETILLO WAS BORN in Aceribo, Puerto Rico to unmarried, working-class parents who encouraged her exploration of revolutionary ideas from a young age. She attended school, but it was her informal education, reading radical works, that formed her political consciousness and anarchist identity. Capetillo joined the labor movement and began working with *La Federación de Torcedores de Tabaco* (The Federation of Tobacco Rollers), as a *lectora* (reader) in a cigar factory. The reader was a highly esteemed role in the culture of tobacco factories, a person hired by the workers to provide entertainment and education through the reading of newspapers and books, often providing material for political debate and discussion.

Capetillo wrote articles for radical labor and union newspapers and authored her own feminist newspaper, a utopian novel, popular plays and what is considered one of the earliest feminist Latina manifestos: *Mi Opinión sobre las Libertades, Derechos y Deberes de la Mujer, como Compañera, Madre y ser Independiente* (*My Opinion on the Liberties, Rights, and Duties of Woman, as Companion, Mother, and Independent Being*). She organized within labor communities, supported strikes, advocated for the rights of women and challenged the hierarchical structures she found existing within social movements. Capetillo lived and traveled in numerous cities in the U.S., the Dominican Republic, France, England and Cuba (where she was arrested for wearing pants in 1915) espousing her continuously evolving belief in labor struggles, progressive education, free love, vegetarianism, universal workers' suffrage and the emancipation of women.

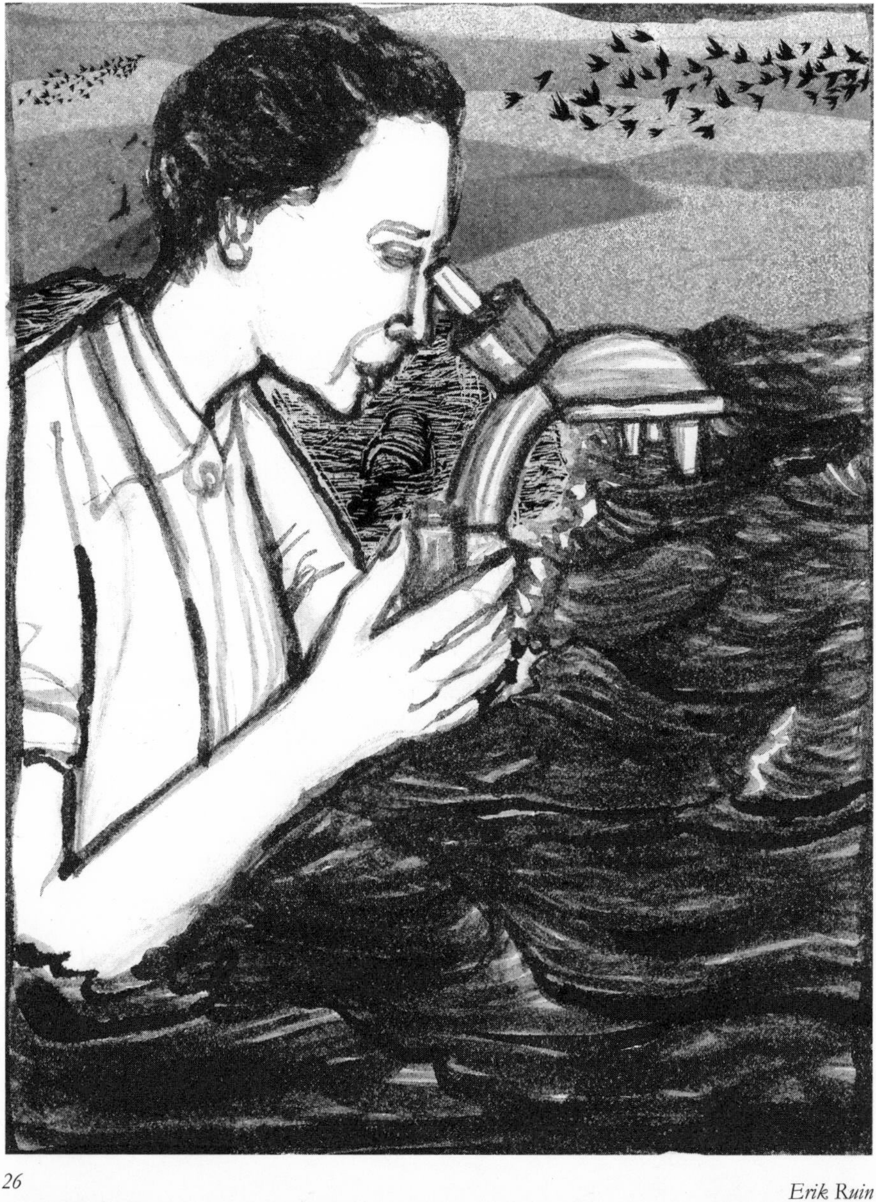

Erik Ruin

Rachel Carson

"The more clearly we can focus our attention on the wonders and realities of the universe about us, the less taste we shall have for destruction."

BORN ON A FAMILY farm near Pittsburgh, Pennsylvania, and educated in small rural schools, Rachel Carson spent much of her childhood exploring the ecosystem around her home. A writer from a young age, her earliest work was in the field of marine biology. Her second book, the poetic *The Sea Around Us*, was her first to achieve bestseller status in 1951.

Carson's work is widely credited with inspiring the modern environmental movement, and her lyrical prose shines in her books on marine ecosystems. However, her best-known work remains *Silent Spring*, which decried the harmful effects of pesticides on the environment, with a particular focus on the dangers of the insecticide DDT. Her campaign against the over-use of pesticides and herbicides led her into direct conflict with the chemical industries and free-market advocates. Published in 1962, *Silent Spring* was widely well-received despite a massive campaign against the book from industry giants Monsanto, DuPont, Velsicol, American Cyanamid and others. Carson died of complications from cancer and radiation therapy in 1964, after seeing at least the beginning of the impact her book would have on the world. DDT was banned by the Environmental Protection Agency in 1972.

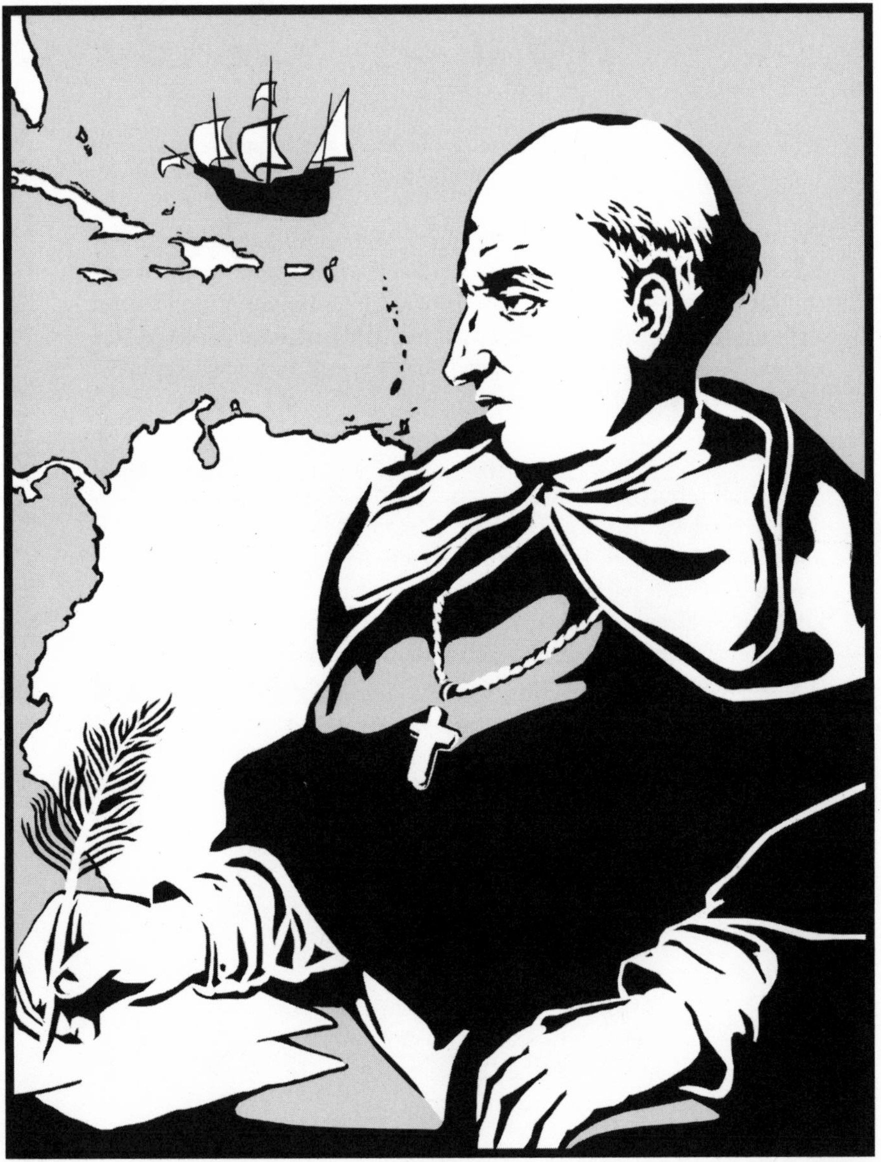

Kristine Virsis

Bartolomé de las Casas

"My eyes have seen these acts so foreign to human nature, and now I tremble as I write."

AT THE AGE OF nine, Bartolomé de las Casas witnessed Christopher Columbus' return to Spain from his first voyage. From what is now called the Bahamas, Columbus brought back seven kidnapped Taíno natives. By 1513, Casas had immigrated to the Caribbean, where he served as a chaplain during the Spanish invasion of Cuba and was given an *encomienda*, a tract of land, complete with its original, now enslaved, inhabitants. Even though he was a part of the conquest of the area, he became increasingly troubled by the brutal treatment of many Indigenous people at the hands of the new settlers, particularly the exportation of slaves, a source of financial income for Columbus, and the destruction of Taíno family relations through forced mineral mining in their homeland.

As an ordained priest, Casas spoke openly against the way the Spanish treated the Indigenous, now subjugated, communities in the Caribbean. He gave up his *encomienda* and traveled back to Spain in hopes of making change at the source. After an unsuccessful attempt at founding a utopian abolitionist colony in Venezuela, Casas began to focus on his theological studies and producing anti-slavery writings. Alongside his abolitionist writings, he continued to push for peaceful conversion of natives in the "New World" to Christianity, and repented his one-time proposal to introduce African slaves to the Caribbean colonies. His efforts at dismantling the Spanish slave trade helped pass the highly contested "New Laws," adopted in 1550, ending the *encomienda* system. Today, Casas' transcriptions of Columbus' journals and other writings are the premier firsthand source of information about the wake of Columbus' expeditions, yet are also seen as the foundation for the demonizing "Black Legend," a highly influential and stereotypical depiction of Spaniards that still resonates.

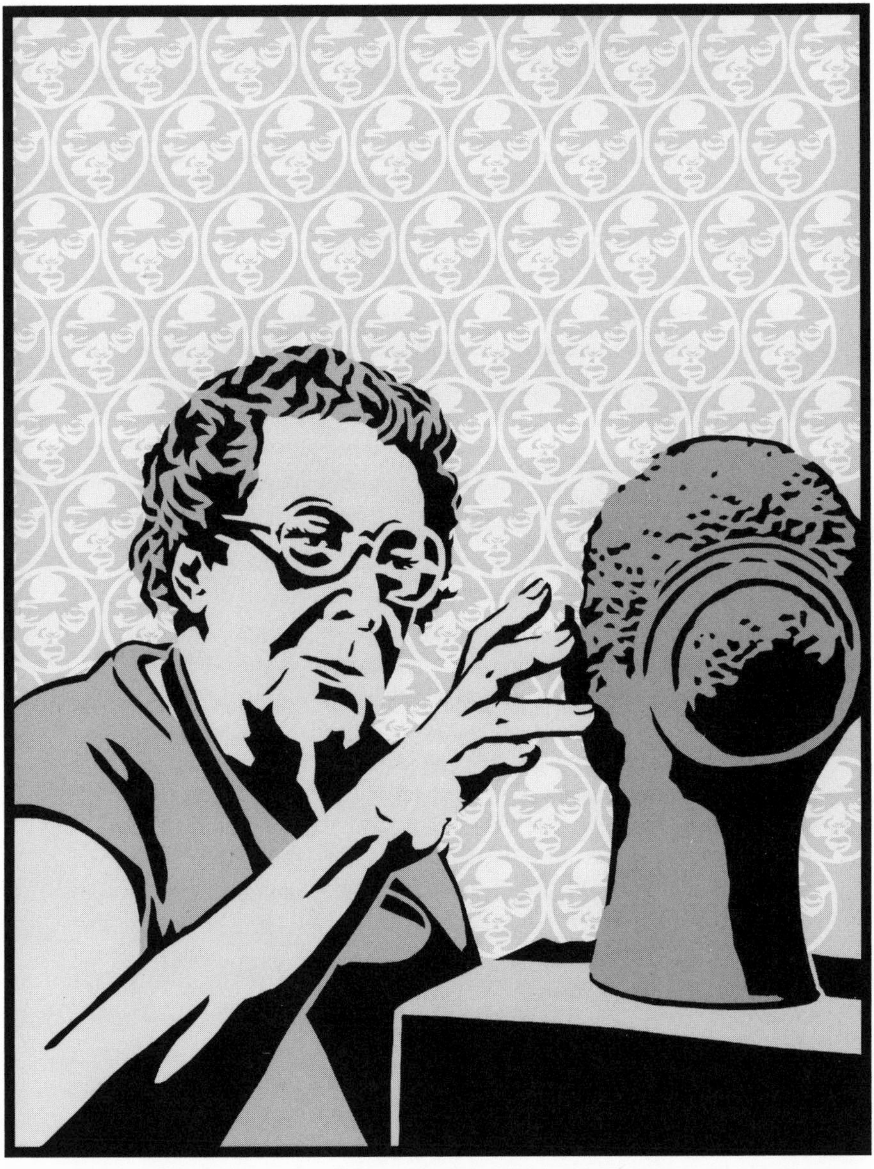

Kristine Virsis

Elizabeth Catlett

"Art is only important to the extent that it aids in the liberation of our people."

ELIZABETH CATLETT IS AN African-American artist who has been working in Mexico since the 1940s, making a life's work of socially charged printmaking and sculpture. Catlett found her voice at a young age, during an anti-lynching protest while in high school in Washington D.C., when she and others were forcibly removed by police from the steps of the Supreme Court building, wearing nooses around their necks. She was active in anti-war and anti-fascist groups at Howard University and was the first African-American student to receive a Master of Fine Arts degree in Sculpture from the University of Iowa.

With few African-American artists to look to for direction, Catlett worked with what she knew. Her prints portray the fears, struggles and pride of ordinary black people through simple and clear emotional imagery. Her portraits of mothers and black heroes combine dignity with tenderness, strength with proud love. Asserting that abstract art has its roots in Africa, Catlett also creates sculptures that recall Pre-Hispanic and West African objects, which function, beyond aesthetic purposes, for social and religious use.

In Mexico, Catlett worked with the politically charged graphics group *Taller de Gráfica Popular* (People's Graphic Arts Workshop) for 20 years alongside her husband, Francisco Mora. With the rise of Black Power movements in the U.S. in the 1960s, Catlett was barred from entering the States until 1971. She continues to work from her home in Cuernavaca, Mexico.

Roberto Clemente

was simply a man, a man who strove to achieve his dream of peace and justice for oppressed people throughout the world."

— from Clemente's obituary in the Black Panther newspaper

Colin Matthes

Roberto Clemente

BORN NEAR THE CANEBRAKES of rural Carolina, Puerto Rico, Roberto Clemente grew up with a passion for playing baseball. He eventually travelled to the United States, where he was drafted by the Pittsburgh Pirates in 1954. In a time where there were virtually no people of color playing organized ball in the U.S., Clemente went on to become the first Latino star in the major leagues and spoke out on the way racism in the U.S. affected Latino athletes.

Clemente's motto was, "if you have a chance to help others and fail to do so, you are wasting your time on this earth." He routinely visited sick children in National League cities; the hospital visits were rarely publicized, but ailing kids everywhere seemed to know about them. Clemente sorted out his large pile of mail in the clubhouse before each road trip and made a special stack for children in cities where the Pirates were headed next.

Two days before Christmas in 1972, a massive earthquake leveled Managua, Nicaragua and killed thousands of residents. Due to the greed of Anastasio Somoza, the Nicaraguan military leader who had the support of the Nixon administration, much of the charitable aid being funneled from the U.S. to Managua failed to reach its destination. Using his fame to draw attention to the situation, Clemente decided to go to Managua in person to make sure food and medical supplies from Puerto Rico reached the people who needed help. Because of the urgency of the situation, he boarded an unsafe, ramshackle plane overloaded with relief supplies. His plane went down over the ocean soon after lift-off, and Roberto's body was never recovered. In 1973, Clemente became the first Latino to be inducted into the Baseball Hall of Fame. Over 40 public schools, two hospitals and a major bridge in Pittsburgh bear his name.

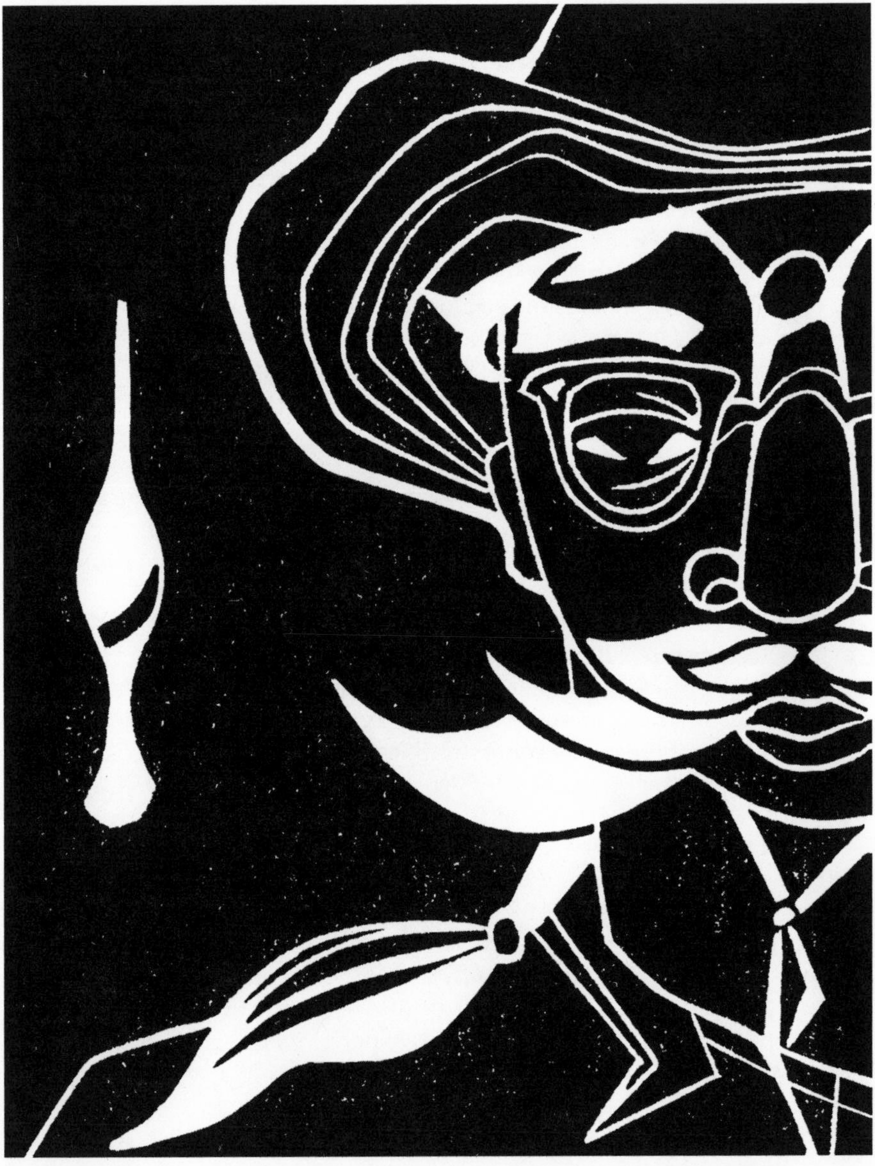

Favianna Rodriguez

"An idea does not become trapped in one person. If the person has an idea and does not give it freedom, it will escape to someone who will."

CARLOS CORTÉZ KOYOKUIKATL WAS born in Milwaukee to radical activist parents. His mother was a German-American socialist pacifist and his father a Mexican-Indian organizer with the Industrial Workers of the World (IWW). His parents raised him in a non-doctrinaire environment and went to great lengths to support his artistry as they nurtured him through the Great Depression. In 1944, Cortéz was drafted but refused to serve in World War II on political grounds. He served two years in federal prison as a conscientious objector.

Carlos Cortéz was a printmaker, poet, anarchist, journalist, songwriter and international political activist who developed powerful, political graphics that celebrated the rights of workers: from campesinos in the fields, to indigenous laborers in Bolivia, to steel workers in the U.S. In 1947, Cortéz joined the IWW and developed some of his best-known linoleum block portraits of labor struggle leaders, including Joe Hill, Lucy Parsons, and Ben Fletcher. Cortéz is the only artist of the IWW whose work has exhibited at the Museum of Modern Art in New York. An anti-capitalist who viewed his art as a tool for justice, he left a provision in his estate in which he requested that "if any of my graphic works are selling for high prices immediate copies should be made to keep the price down."

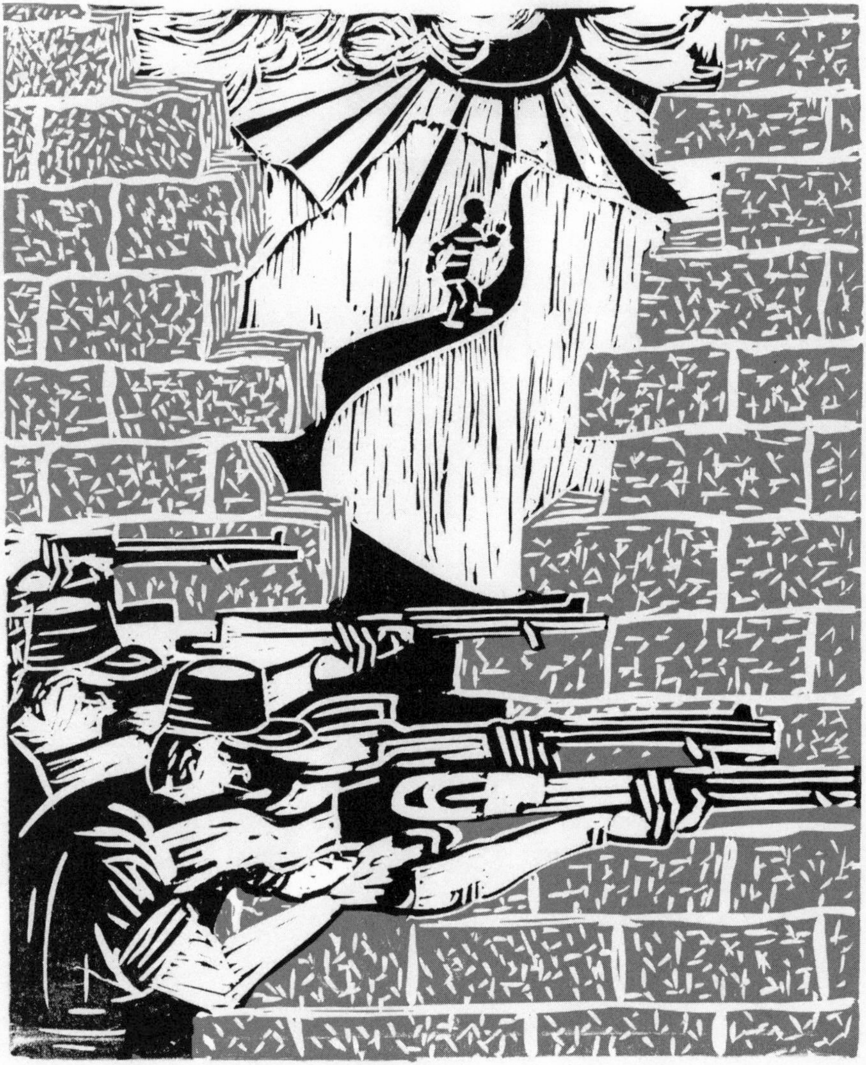

Josh MacPhee

Roque Dalton (signature)

BORN IN THE **1930s**, Roque Dalton joined the Communist Party of El Salvador at an early age and was educated in both his homeland and Mexico. He was deeply committed to the political power of art, especially poetry. By the 1960s, he had been arrested multiple times for his political organizing. He miraculously escaped death by firing squad while imprisoned in 1965, when an earthquake destroyed the walls of his cell and allowed him to escape. Dalton lived in exile in Mexico and Cuba and traveled extensively in the Communist world, including time in Vietnam, Korea and the Soviet Union. He wrote many books of poetry and essays focused on human liberation, in particular the liberation of the people of El Salvador. In 1974, he returned to El Salvador and immediately went underground, helping to found the People's Revolutionary Army (ERP). Because of his clandestine return and involvement with the guerillas, Dalton could no longer write poetry under his own name and wrote dozens of poems under a series of pseudonyms, now known as the _Poemas Clandestinos_. In 1975, Dalton was captured, tortured and murdered, but his poems have only gained popularity, and continue to communicate his love of art, working-class people and his homeland.

"Like you I
love love, life, the sweet smell
of things, the sky-
blue landscape of January days.

And my blood boils up
and I laugh through eyes
that have known the buds of tears.
I believe the world is beautiful
and that poetry, like bread,
is for everyone.

And that my veins don't end in me
but in the unanimous blood
of those who struggle for life,
love,
little things,
landscape and bread,
the poetry of everyone."

–"Like You," Roque Dalton
(translated by Jack Hirschman), 1975

Let my final actions thunder of love, solidarity, protest—of empowerment. I adamantly protest the richest culture in the history of the world, a culture which has the obvious potential to create a golden age of science and democracy dedicated to maximizing the quality of life of every person, but which still squanders the majority of its human and physical capital on modern versions of primitive symbols of power and prestige.

Kevin Caplicki

Justin Dart, Jr.

JUSTIN DART, JR. GREW up in a wealthy Chicago home. His father had married into the Walgreen family and went on to preside over his own Dart Industries. Raised with an upper-class education and little paternal affection, Dart rebelled against his upbringing, and became an angry and contemptuous teenager. At 18, Dart contracted polio, and although he was told he only had a few days to live, he survived with the help of hospital staff whose nurturing spirits had a profound effect.

Recovered but reliant on a wheelchair, Dart sought a new life, melding his privileged upbringing with a newfound desire for a compassionate lifestyle. He worked on various successful global corporate ventures while struggling with drug and alcohol abuse until a 1968 visit with children with stricken by polio in Saigon jolted Dart to his core. After witnessing squalid and destitute conditions and identifying personal culpability, Dart and his lifetime partner Yoshiko went into self-imposed exile and reflection in rural Japan. After six years, they returned to the U.S. and dove headlong into full political activism on behalf of people with disabilities.

Passionate about radical changes to the law and working to directly agitate within the political system, Justin Dart, Jr. advocated full civil rights for people with disabilities and a new culture of love and empowerment. Through his passionate work and popular influence, he was brought on board several presidential organizations during the Reagan and H.W. Bush administrations. He is best remembered as a primary organizer in the creation and passing of the Americans with Disabilities Act of 1990 (ADA). Dart received the Presidential Medal of Freedom in 1998.

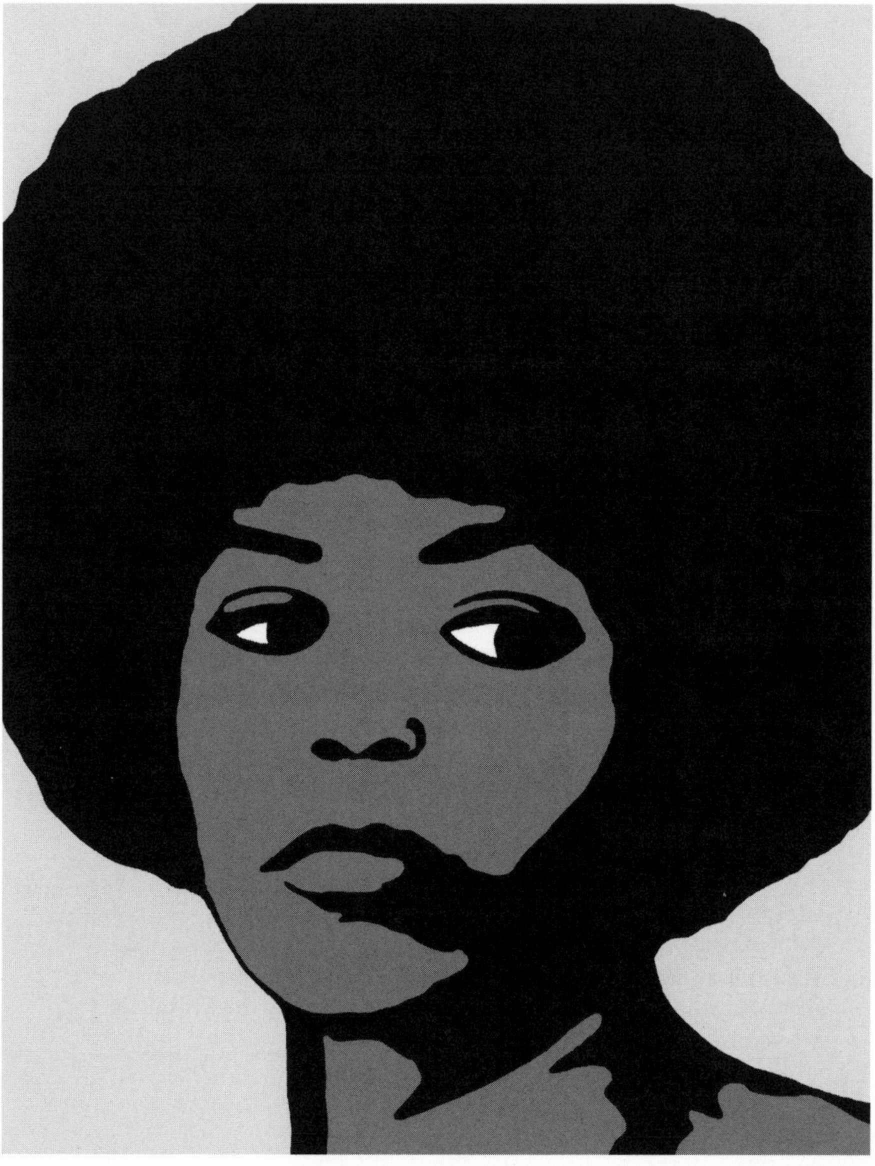

Jesus Barraza

Angela Y. Davis

"Radical simply means 'grasping things at the root.'"

ORIGINALLY FROM BIRMINGHAM, ALABAMA, Angela Yvonne Davis is a scholar, orator and revolutionary. Davis became involved with the Black Panther Party in the summer of 1970, working on a campaign to free imprisoned Black Panther activists the Soledad Brothers. When a shotgun registered in Davis' name was used in an attempt to free prisoner James McClain during a court hearing (an action committed in hopes of gaining support for the release of the Soledad Brothers), Davis appeared on the FBI's "Ten Most Wanted" list and was thrust into the national spotlight. Davis fled California and was apprehended two months later in New York City. A campaign to get her out of prison was established, and the cause spread around the world. After she was acquitted of all charges, Davis traveled to Cuba.

Previously a member of the Communist Party, Angela Davis ran for vice president of the United States along with Gus Hall in 1980 and 1984. During the 1980s, she became strongly involved in the prison abolition movement, working to end the prison-industrial complex and abolish the death penalty. Davis is now a graduate Professor Emeritus in the History of Consciousness program at University of California Santa Cruz, and works with Critical Resistance, an organization dedicated to the idea of the abolition of prisons as a fundamental step towards social justice. She has written numerous books and continues to publish.

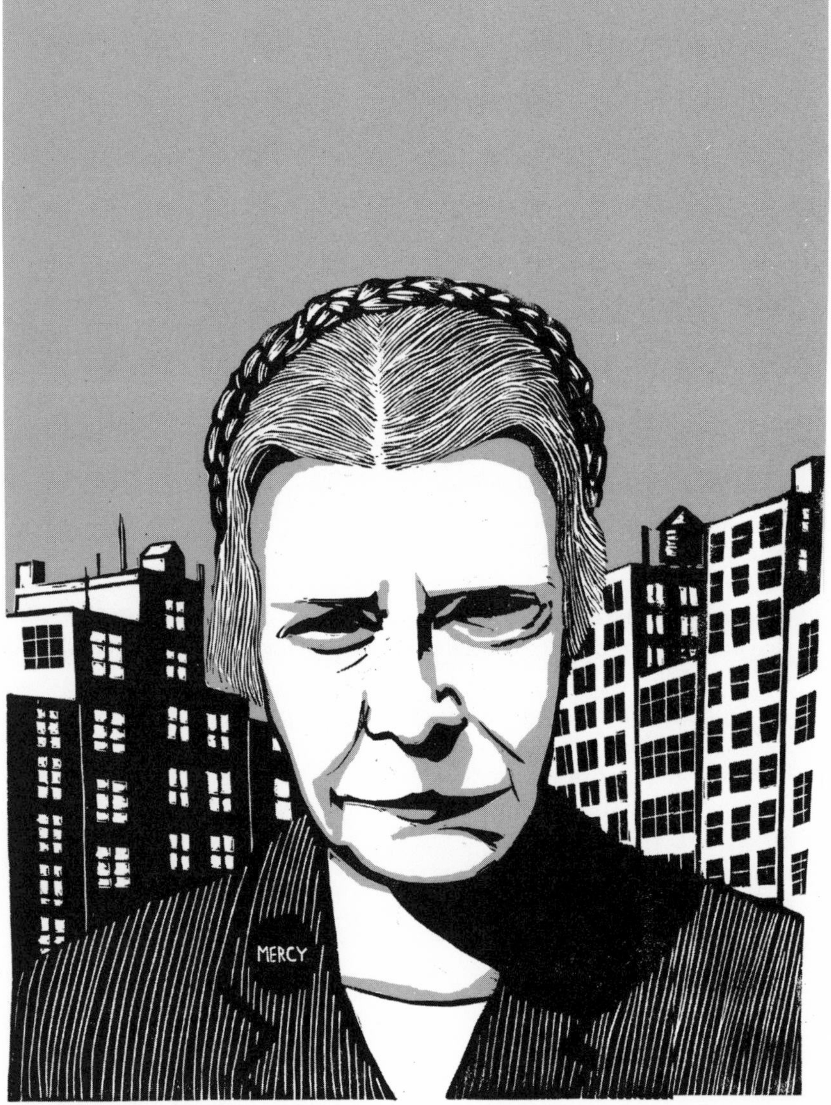
MERCY

Alec "Icky" Dunn

Dorothy Day

"The class structure is our making and by our consent, not God's, and we must do what we can to change it. We are urging revolutionary change."

BORN INTO AN UPPER-MIDDLE-CLASS family, Dorothy Day dropped out of college midway through her studies and moved to New York City, insistent on supporting herself. There, she hung out with well-known bohemians of the time, worked on leftist and socialist newspapers and pursued a career in writing. Day converted to Catholicism in 1927, following a period of spiritual awakening leading up to the birth of her daughter, Tamar. Blending her beliefs in social justice, anarchism and faith, she found the problems of poverty to be a religious mystery and began to work for social equality as a radical Catholic. In particular, she was a steadfast proponent of pacifist, nonviolent direct action and civil disobedience, a stance that would see her labeled an iconoclast within the Catholic Church.

Dorothy Day founded the Catholic Worker movement with fellow activist Peter Maurin. The Catholic Workers, a decentralized organization that today functions in some 185 international communities, is dedicated to radical Christian activism; protesting war, racism and injustice and advocating for nonviolence, voluntary poverty, direct aid for the homeless and hungry and pacifist direct action. Catholic Worker houses are active in urban as well as rural settings, where people are given shelter to live and work communally. Controversially, Dorothy Day has been under consideration for sainthood in the Catholic Church, although she herself had said, "Don't call me a saint. I don't want to be dismissed so easily."

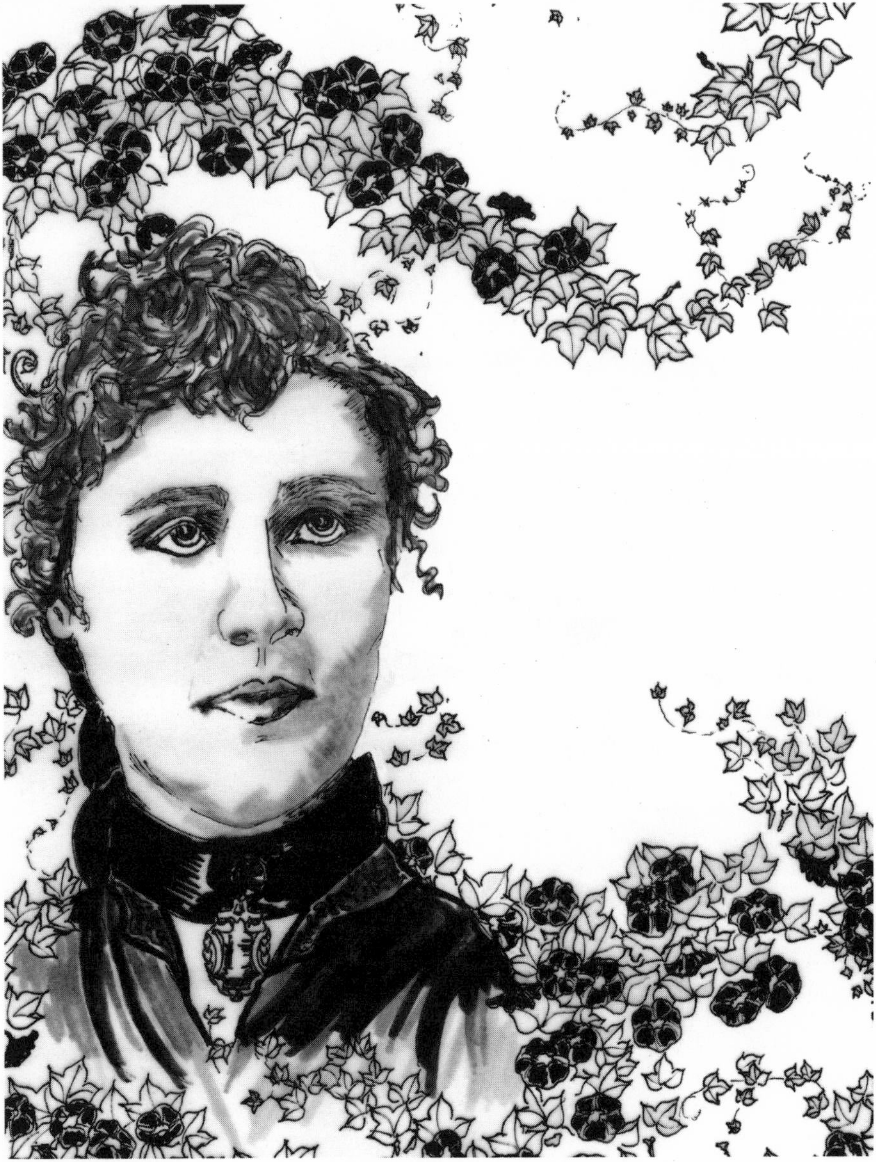

Voltairine De Cleyre

"Anarchism, to me, means not only the denial of authority, not only a new economy, but a revision of the principles of morality."

VOLTAIRINE DE CLEYRE WAS born in Leslie, Michigan and lived much of her life in extreme poverty. Her family had ties to the abolitionist movement and she was named after the philosopher Voltaire, whom her father admired for his free thought. De Cleyre was sent to a convent during her high school years, initiating her anti-authoritarian ideals at an early age. The execution of the Haymarket martyrs in Chicago in 1887 inspired de Cleyre, like so many other young American radicals, to proclaim herself an anarchist and commit her life to liberation movements.

De Cleyre involved herself in teaching Jewish immigrant communities, speaking at labor meetings and organizing funds for the Mexican Revolution. Her belief in "anarchism without adjectives" made a plea for cooperation amongst anarchist factions. Well-known for her talents as a writer and lecturer, she was called the "rebel poet" and "the most gifted and brilliant anarchist woman America ever produced" by her contemporary Emma Goldman. Plagued by depression and ill health most of her life, she attempted suicide on two occasions and survived an assassination attempt by a former student in 1902. Her literary legacy, however, includes poetry, stories and essays on subjects such as individual free will, the emancipation of women, education, direct action, nature, liberty and justice, and on whole radiate with hope for a just world.

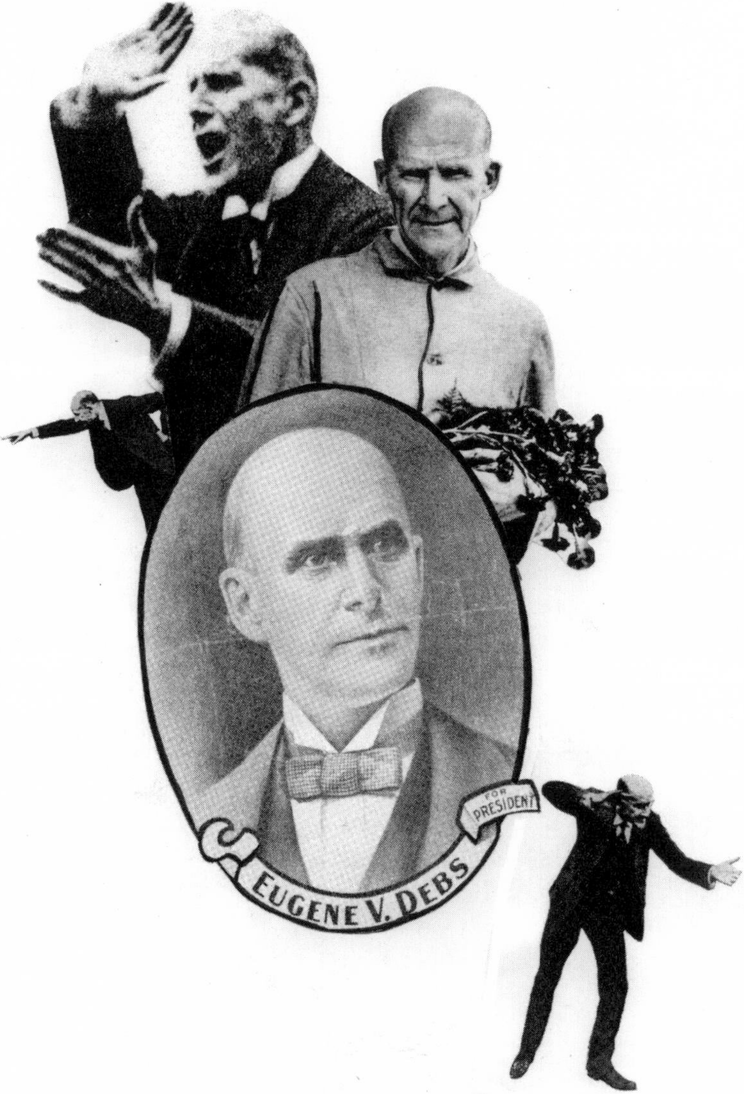
FOR
PRESIDENT
EUGENE V. DEBS

Eugene V. Debs

"While there is a lower class, I am in it. While there is a criminal element,
I am of it. While there is a soul in prison, I am not free."

THE NAME EUGENE DEBS is synonymous with socialism
and the American left at the turn of the 20th century in the United States. As a young man, Debs rose quickly in the ranks of the
Brotherhood of Locomotive Fireman, but became convinced that
unionized workers should develop more confrontational tactics to
challenge their subservient relationship to management. In 1893, he
founded the American Railway Union (ARU), the first industrial union (as opposed to traditional craft-based unions). One year later, the
ARU led a strike against the Pullman Railway Car Company outside
of Chicago, which became one of the most famous and heated strikes
in U.S. history, eventually involving 250,000 workers in 27 states.

Debs served six months in jail for leading the Pullman Strike. While
imprisoned he read Marx, and turned his focus towards socialist organizing within the working class in the U.S. He helped found the
Industrial Workers of the World (IWW) in 1905, and as a political
candidate he ran for president five times under the Socialist Party of
America. His most famous campaign was conducted in 1920 while
he served time in Atlanta Federal Penitentiary, sentenced at age 63 to
10 years under the Espionage Act. He received over 900,000 votes;
campaign buttons read, "Vote for Prisoner 9653."

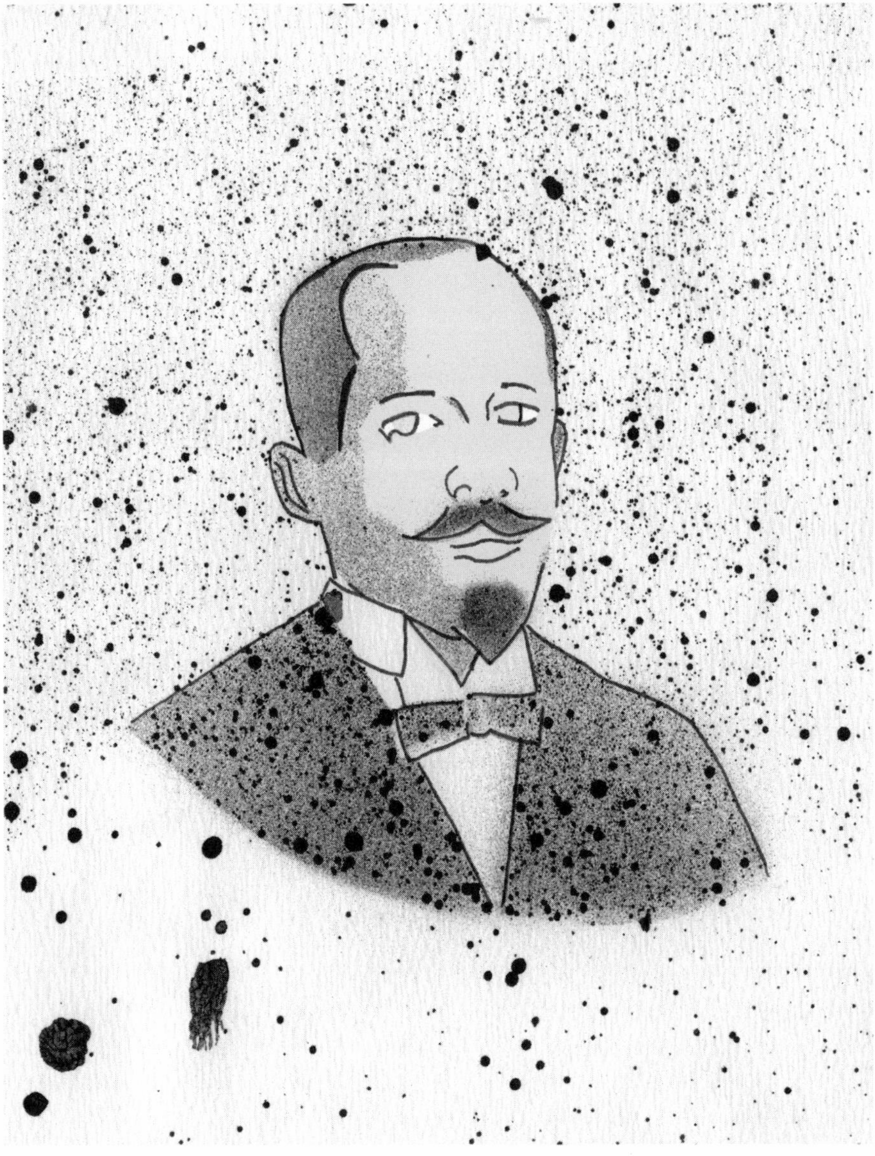

Kevin Caplicki

W.E.B. Du Bois

"Present-day students are often puzzled at the apparent contradictions of Southern slavery. One hears, on the one hand, of the staid and gentle patriarchy, the wide and sleepy plantations with lord and retainers, ease and happiness; on the other hand one hears of barbarous cruelty and unbridled power and wide oppression of men. Which is the true picture? The answer is simple: Both are true. They are not opposite sides of the same shield; they are different shields."

WILLIAM EDWARD BURGHARDT DU BOIS was undeniably one of the most prominent voices for racial justice in the first half of the 20th century. Considered by many to be the father of Pan-Africanism, Du Bois was of mixed racial heritage and from a young age was a headstrong intellectual and writer. He excelled in his studies at Fisk University in Nashville and went on to become the first African-American to earn a Ph.D. from Harvard. An educator, criminologist, sociologist and activist, Du Bois left a legacy of celebrated books including *The Souls of Black Folk*, *The Negro*, and a biography of John Brown of which he was particularly proud.

W.E.B. Du Bois often found himself at odds with other black intellectuals and leaders on issues of segregation and assimilation into "American" culture. His writings heavily criticized the foundational white supremacy of the United States, dissolving the notion that there was a scientific explanation for racism. Du Bois was part of the formation of the National Association for the Advancement of Colored People (NAACP), and was at the helm of their publication *The Crisis* for 25 years. Du Bois held controversial views on eugenics and birth control, and attracted the attention of the FBI for his staunch support of Stalin's Russia. He spent the last two years of his life working in Ghana.

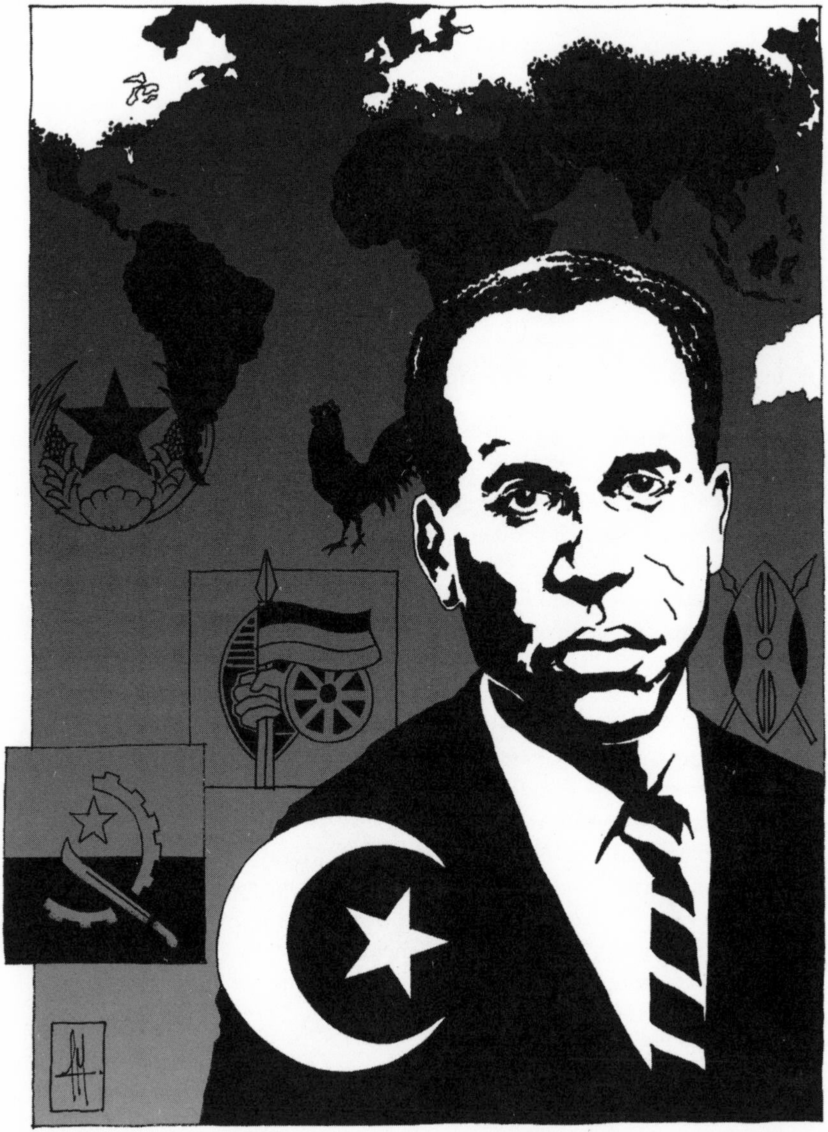

Fernando Marti

Frantz Fanon

"He who is reluctant to recognize me opposes me."

FRANTZ FANON WAS A psychiatrist and anti-colonial revolutionary from Martinique whose writings have inspired anti-colonial liberation movements for the past 40 years. His first book, *Black Skin, White Masks*, published in 1952, was an analysis of the effect of colonial subjugation and the psychological inadequacy felt by oppressed populations in relation to their colonizers. His widely circulated *The Wretched of the Earth* constitutes a warning to the oppressed of Algeria (and indeed, the rest of the world) about the dangers they face in the process of decolonization and in the transition to a neo-colonialist world. *Wretched* emphasizes the need for native populations to have educational practices that are not just an extension of the colonial culture that they live under, but rather reflect the populations' own cultures and values.

Following the outbreak of the Algerian revolution in November 1954, Fanon joined the resistance army *Front de Libération Nationale* (FLN) and worked as both a therapist for Algerian rebels and a clandestine war strategist. Some of his most salient and timeless writings concern what he saw as the necessity for revolutionary violence to overthrow colonial oppression. In the case of the French occupation of Algeria, for example, Fanon argued that if an Algerian experience of occupation is understood as permanent because of the threat of violence, then it is only possible for resistance to happen through this same language of violence. Fanon's writing have often come under criticism for their hetero-normative and masculine-centered viewpoint, yet his critiques and theories on violence and psychological decolonization have continued to have lasting influence on global liberation movements.

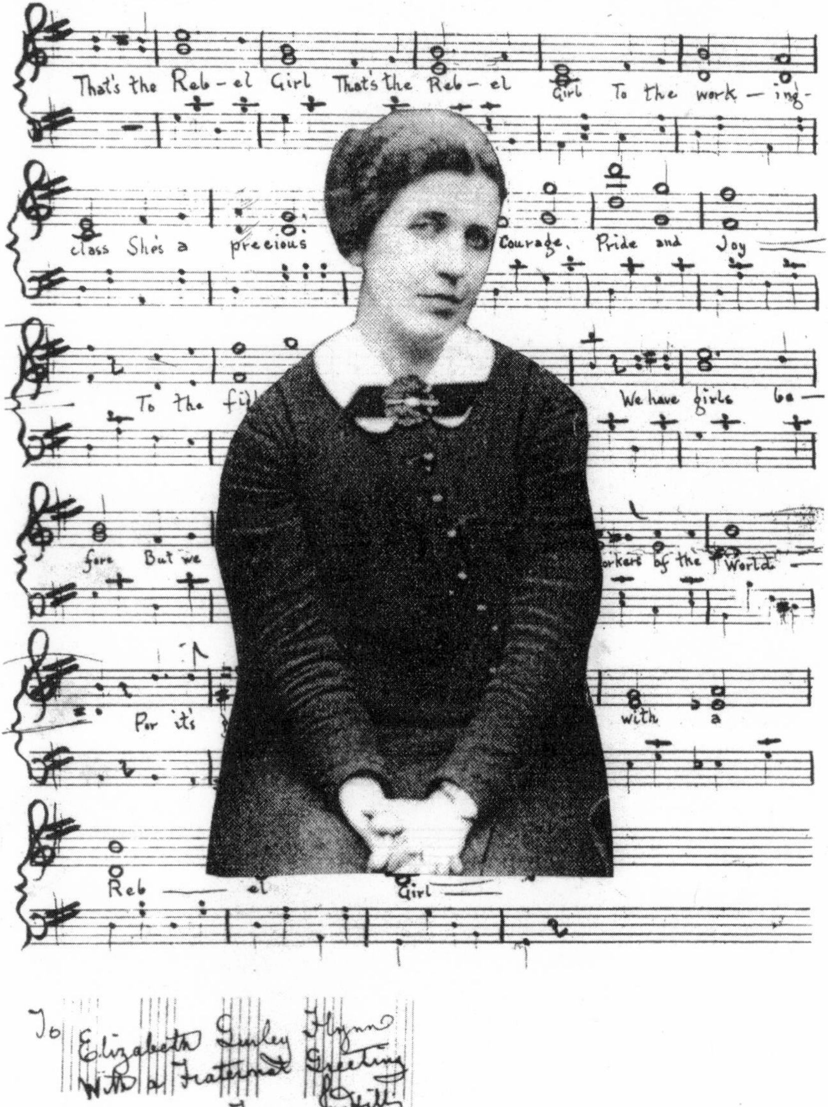
That's the Reb - el Girl That's the Reb - el Girl To the work - ing -
class She's a precious
Courage, Pride and Joy
To the
We have girls be -
fore But we
of the World
For it's
with a
Reb - el Girl
To Elizabeth Gurley Flynn
With a Fraternal Greeting
From Joe Hill

Nicolas Lampert

Elizabeth Gurley Flynn

"What is a labor victory? I maintain that it is a twofold thing. Workers must gain economic advantage, but they must also gain revolutionary spirit, in order to achieve a complete victory. For workers to gain a few cents more a day, a few minutes less a day, and go back to work with the same psychology, the same attitude toward society, is to achieve a temporary gain and not a lasting victory."

KNOWN FOREVER AS THE "Rebel Girl" after Joe Hill dedicated his song to her, Elizabeth Gurley Flynn devoted her life to working class struggles and women's rights. Flynn was born in Concord, New Hampshire, grew up in poverty in the South Bronx, and at age 16, gave her first speech, "What Socialism Will Do for Women" at the Harlem Socialist Club. Shortly after, she joined the Industrial Workers of the World (IWW) and quickly became one the organization's most important strike organizers and speakers. As a Wobbly organizer, Flynn helped direct the IWW free speech fights in Missoula, Montana (1908) and Spokane, Washington (1909-1910), the Lawrence Textile Strike (1912) and the silk workers general strike in Paterson, New Jersey (1913).

A founding member of the American Civil Liberties Union (ACLU), Flynn dedicated much of her social work to woman's rights, birth control and suffrage. She joined the U.S. Communist Party in 1936, and would become the national chairperson 25 years later. Her affiliation with the Communists resulted in her eventual dismissal from the ACLU, and led to her persecution under the Smith Act and a two-year sentence at the women's penitentiary at Alderson, West Virginia. Flynn died in the Soviet Union, and her ashes were brought back to the Waldheim Cemetery outside of Chicago to be buried near the Haymarket martyrs.

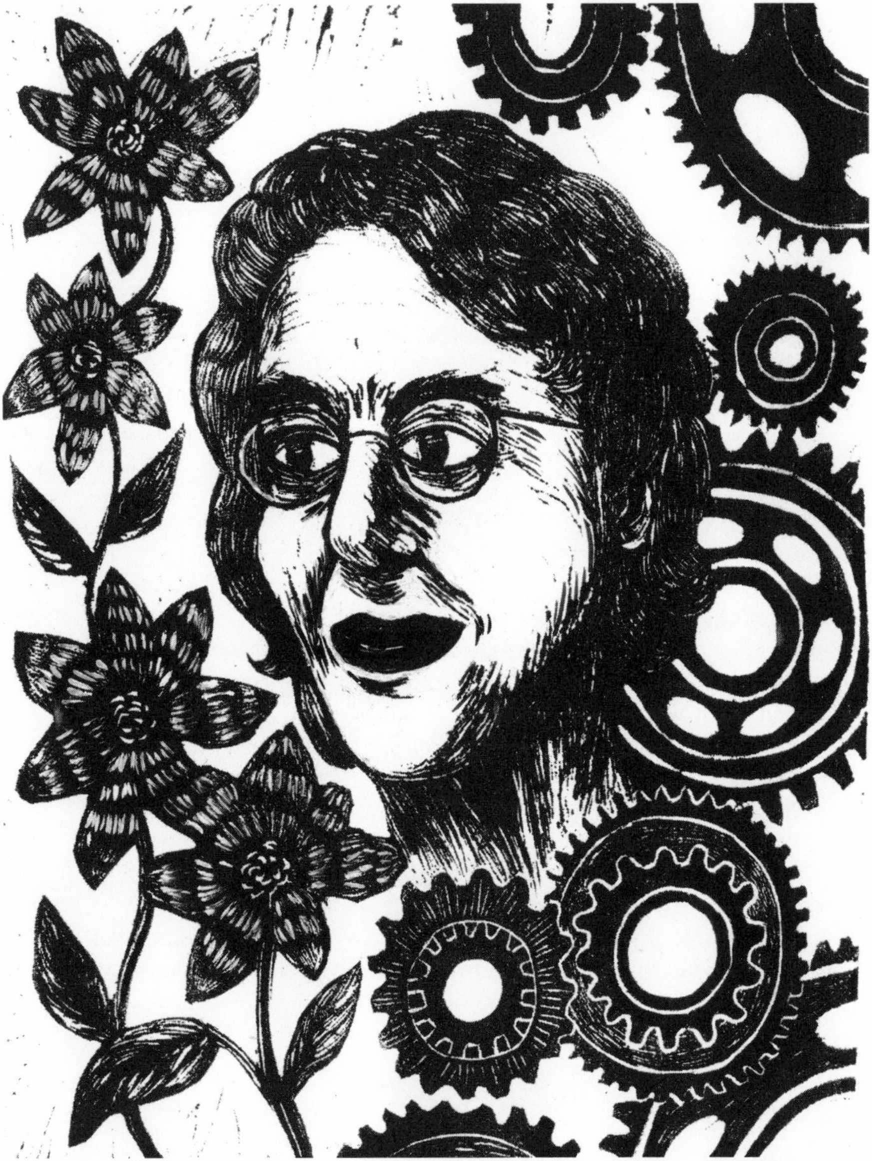

Meredith Stern

Ursula Franklin

"I am more convinced than ever that nothing but the practice of pacifism—the individual and collective conduct by means of care and respect—offers a path into a constructive and creative future."

URSULA WAS BORN IN Munich, and lost many members of her family in Nazi concentration camps during World War II. She received her Ph.D. in experimental physics in Berlin in 1948 and has received several honorary degrees in the years following. Her scientific work has had direct results in practice. Her research assisted in ending atmospheric weapons testing, helped Canadian conscientious objectors redirect their taxes from military contributions towards peaceful purposes and worked to alleviate gender discrimination in the sciences. She has attempted to improve international relations in numerous ways, particularly by travelling to countries during wartime, meeting with women in North Vietnam and the Soviet Union during the Cold War and telling their stories.

Guided by her Quaker background, Franklin believes in practicing consensus-based decision making in worldly and daily living. Her work in science, technology, education, government and public planning is based on the belief that only through a true commitment to non-violence in all human action can we create a just, peaceful and egalitarian world. Franklin's critique of technology is wary of developments that help sustain threat-based hierarchical control systems, the ultimate development of which is militarism. She argues for a holistic approach to technology that encourages critical thinking and positive social and individual impact.

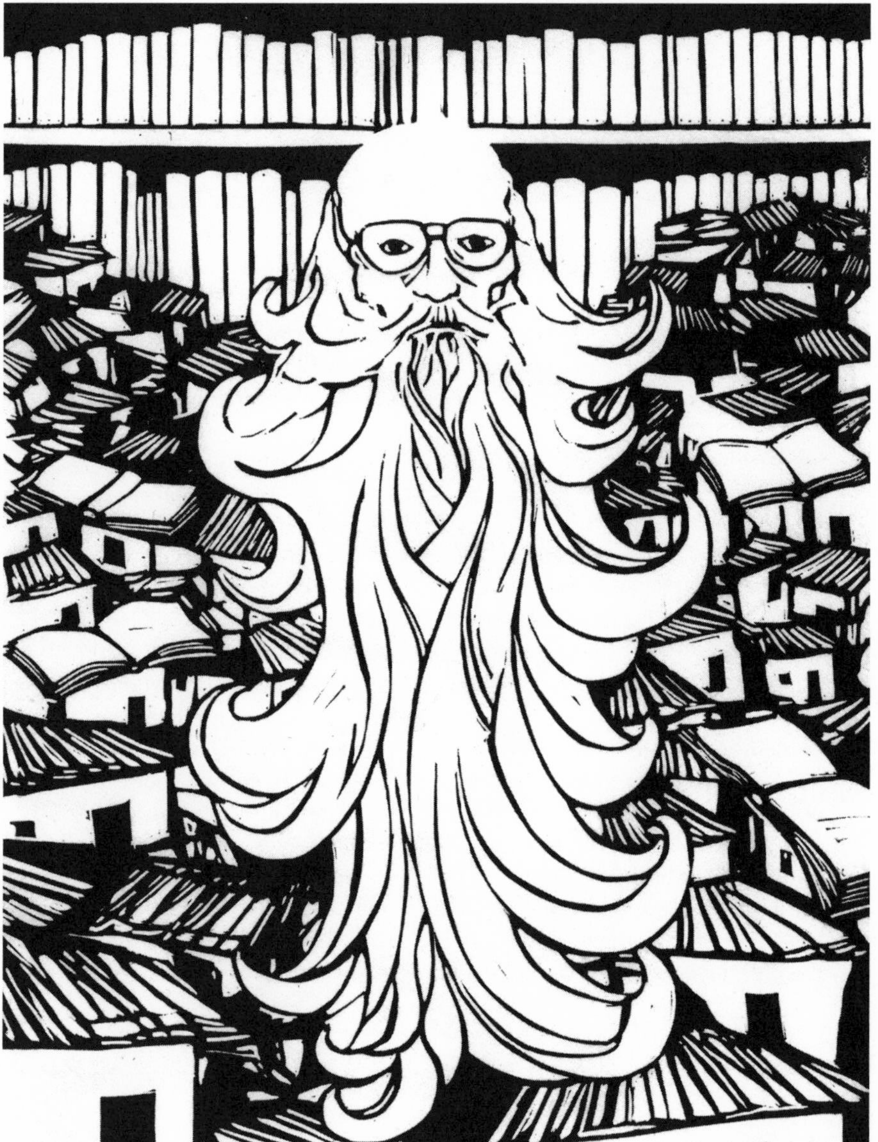

Pete Yahnke

"This is the road I have tried to follow as a teacher: living my convictions; being open to the process of knowing and sensitive to the experience of teaching as an art; being pushed forward by the challenges that prevent me from bureaucratizing my practice; accepting my limitations, yet always conscious of the necessary effort to overcome them and aware that I cannot hide them because to do so would be a failure to respect both my students and myself as a teacher"

PAULO FREIRE WAS A radical Brazilian educator who saw teaching as an inherently political act, arguing that no form of education is neutral and that all teaching is a call to action. In 1961, he put his theories to the test and taught 300 sugarcane workers to read and write in 45 days, consequently making them eligible to vote. In 1964, during a CIA-backed military coup d'état to overthrow Brazilian president Joao Goulart, Freire was imprisoned for over a month for his involvement in state-sponsored literacy programs aimed at assisting two million working-class Brazilians. His brief time in prison served only to solidify his ideas about the relationship between education and politics.

Freire's most influential work, *Pedagogy of the Oppressed*, resulted from his belief that change could only come through an educated population that understood the root problems of domination. In the book, he argues against the traditional dichotomy of the roles of teacher and student. Freire believed that educators should allow for space wherein they could continue to learn from the learner, and embrace critiques of dominant power at the core of their curriculums. He particularly despised the "banking" notion in education, where the teacher fills each student's mind with facts as though it were previously an empty account. The student, he believed, should experience truth as social understanding, not as a pre-determined plateau arbitrated by standardized testing.

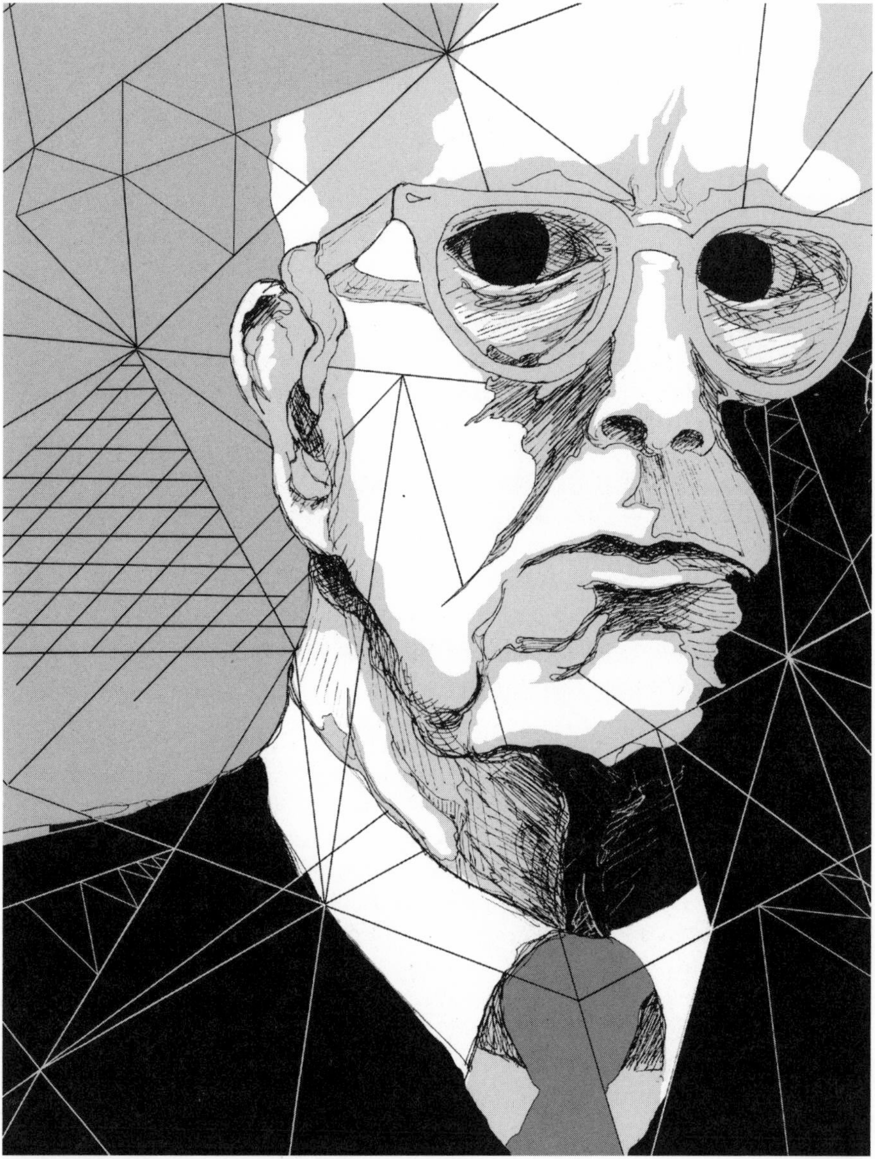

Pete Yahnke

Buckminster Fuller

"The Things To Do Are: the things that need doing, that you see need to be done, and that no one else seems to see need to be done. Then you will conceive your own way of doing that which needs to be done—that no one else has told you to do or how to do it. This will bring out the real you that often gets buried inside a character that has acquired a superficial array of behaviors induced or imposed by others on the individual."

RICHARD BUCKMINSTER FULLER WAS a multi-talented individual whose broad impact on design, science and architecture can be difficult to summarize. Highly regarded as a mathematician, philosopher, inventor, architect, artist, Unitarian Universalist, humanist and futurist, Fuller was awarded 28 U.S. patents for his various ideas and inventions. Most well known is the geodesic dome, a model form that has been used continuously and re-interpreted globally. Praised and admired for his ideas, Buckminster Fuller (known colloquially as "Bucky"), is also appreciated for his perceived quirkiness and stalwart individualism.

While in his early thirties, Fuller and his wife Anne lost their young daughter. Fuller slipped into despair and alcohol abuse, but eventually arose to face a new self-imposed lifestyle experiment: "to find what a single individual could contribute to changing the world and benefiting all humanity." Fuller would move rapidly forward from this difficult point in his life to become one of the world's best-known self-educated theorists. His approach to design often saw an attempt to find the best ways to do more by using less resources and increasing overall efficiency, which has made him particularly influential in movements towards environmental sustainability. Fuller optimistically believed in the human capacity for technological innovation, which he thought could harmonize humanity as well as fix socio-economic problems worldwide.

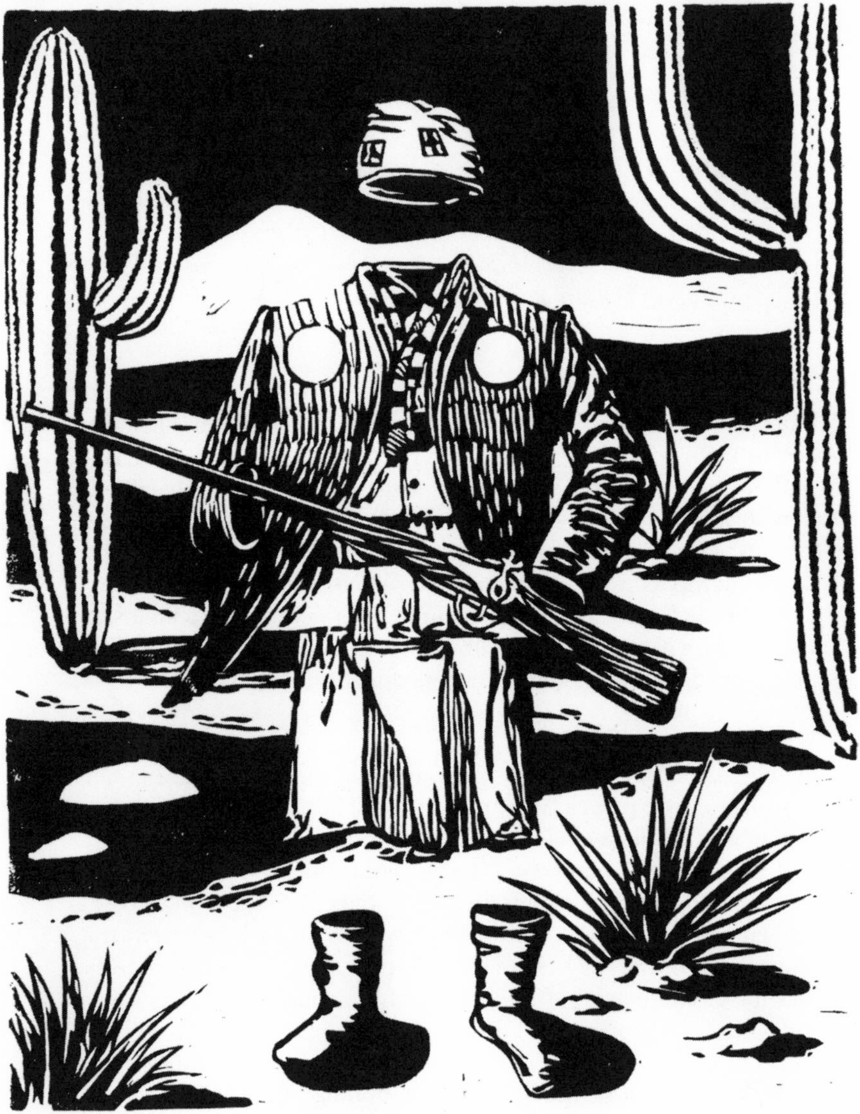

Roger Peet

Geronimo

"If I am killed, no one need mourn for me. My people have all been killed in that country and I, too, will die if need be."

INVISIBLE. IMPLACABLE. UN-KILLABLE. In the eyes of United States settlers, that was the image of the Apache leader Geronimo (Goyahkla), as they colonized the mountainous desert regions of what is now New Mexico and Arizona. The Chiricahua Apaches had developed a reputation as brilliant defenders of their ancestral lands, vengeful spirits whose grit and tenacity matched the harsh desert that raised them. The customary betrayals, lies and thefts perpetrated by the tide of settlers and their military watchdogs brought reprisals from the Apache tribes, and from none more so than the Chiricahuas. Geronimo and his band struck terror into hearts and sowed panic, from their ability to appear from nowhere, strike without mercy and vanish like a dawn mist.

Geronimo inherited his mantle of war leader from the great chiefs that preceded him, Cochise and Victorio. With his band, he fought the armies of Mexico and the U.S. with equal enthusiasm, and evaded capture for decades, slipping back and forth across the border, swooping down from hideouts in the Chiricahua and Sierra Nevada mountains to lay waste to the settlers below. He was the last war leader of his people, and he was waging war against the U.S. government.

Geronimo claimed in life to be un-killable and in truth was wounded over 50 times by bullets. He lived out his later years imprisoned in Indian territory, scarred, defeated and longing always to take back his rifle and return to war against the people who had destroyed his world. His bones are rumored to be in the possession of the Skull and Bones Society of Yale University, a secret fraternal order of wealthy sophisticates who claim among their alumni several U.S. presidents and senators.

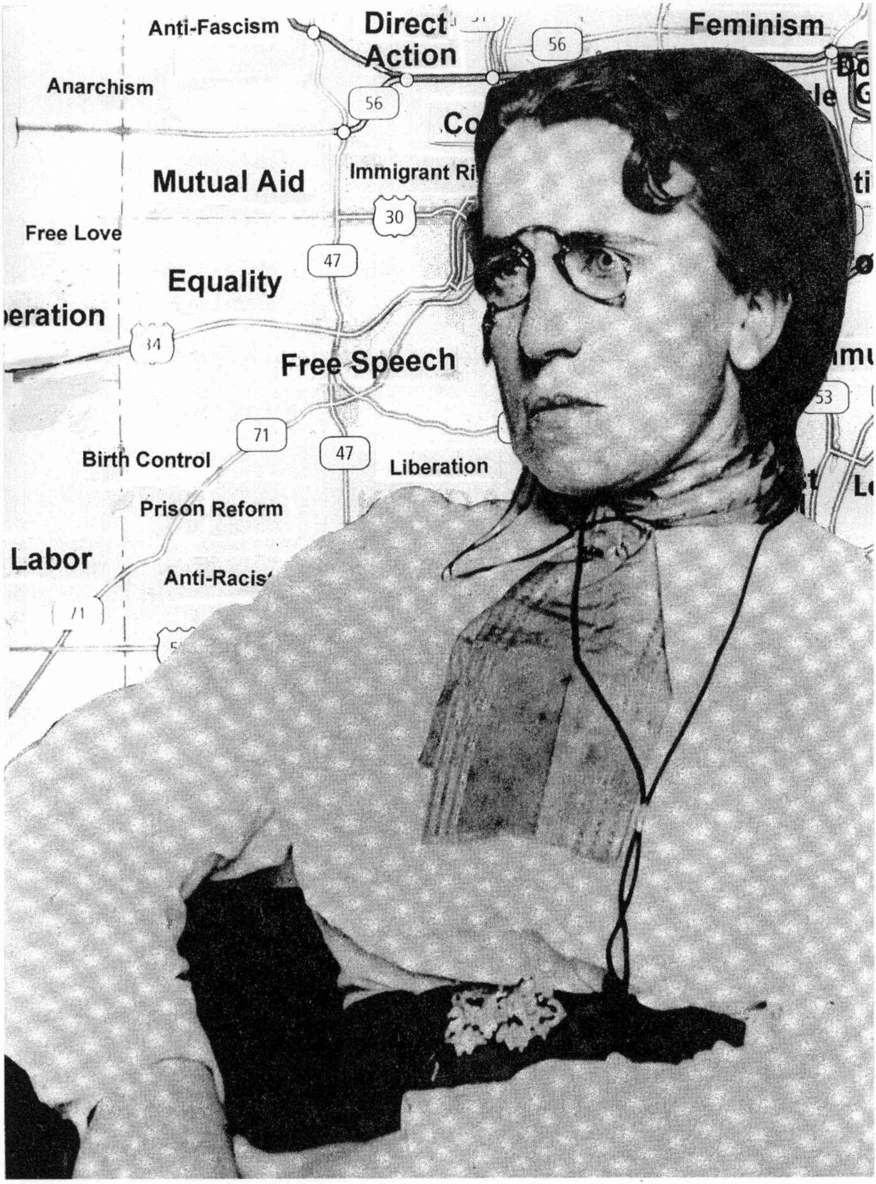
Anti-Fascism
Direct Action
Feminism
Anarchism
Mutual Aid
Free Love
Equality
Free Speech
Birth Control
Liberation
Prison Reform
Labor

Nicolas Lampert

"The most violent element in society is ignorance."

EMMA GOLDMAN HAS BECOME something of an icon of anarchism in North America; her forceful, no-nonsense writings, multi-faceted approach to revolution and militant, passionate life story have inspired generations to rethink the world around them from an anti-authoritarian perspective. Goldman was born in the Russian province of Konvo (now Lithuania) in 1869, and immigrated to the U.S. with her beloved older sister Helena at age 17 in hopes of escaping her unsupportive family. Anarchist literature, socialist meetings and the Haymarket Affair in 1886 deeply radicalized Goldman. She soon became a renowned lecturer on anarchist philosophy, women's rights and social issues such as prison abolition, atheism, militarism, free love and the ills of capitalism. Working as a midwife between speaking tours, her speeches attracted thousands and her publication, *Mother Earth*, became a printed outlet for an entire generation of the radical American Left.

Alongside friend and lover Alexander Berkman, Goldman aided in a failed assassination attempt on industrial magnate Henry Clay Frick, and would be falsely implicated in the killing of President William McKinley by Leon Czolgosz in 1901. She was imprisoned for distributing information about birth control and encouraging men to resist the war draft, and her lectures were so often disrupted by police that she began to carry a book to read in case of her arrest. Along with Berkman, Goldman was deported to Russia in 1919. She would continue to travel, agitating and writing until her health began to fail in 1940.

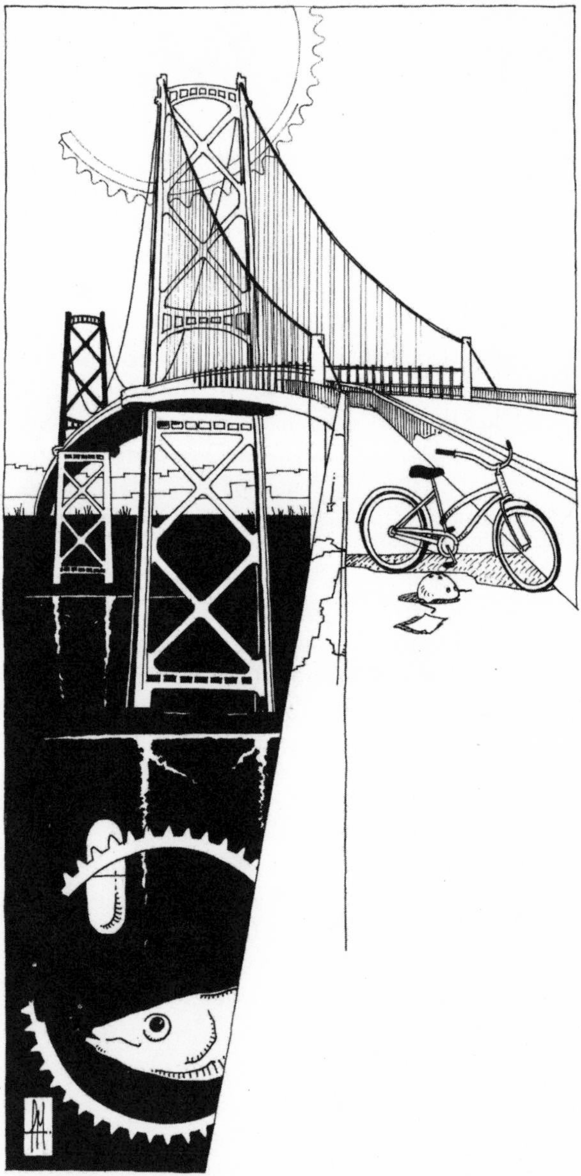

Fernando Marti

Tooker Gomberg

"Take care of ourselves and each other, spend time with loved ones, take breaks when necessary, and enjoy each moment on this lovely green and blue planet."

TOOKER GOMBERG WAS A Canadian environmental and anti-nuclear activist, bicycle advocate and creative agitator whose confrontational tactics were limited only by his time and imagination. Gomberg was especially known for his pranks and direct actions: he locked himself in a vault in the Alberta Premier's office as a protest against the premier's stance on Kyoto, broke into a Netherlands NATO Air Force base that was illegally storing nuclear weapons and in 2000, and organized a group of protesters who threw pennies at the head of Imperial Oil during the company's annual general meeting to make the point that it would cost only pennies per share to reduce greenhouse gases. In Edmonton, Alberta, he headed the EcoCity Society and was elected to Edmonton's city council. Gomberg continued to run for various elections across Canada, not so much with the goal of winning but because of a belief in the galvanizing and educational possibilities of elections, the potential to bring together diverse people around new and progressive ideas.

Like many activists, Gomberg often suffered a deep emotional toll as a result of his idealism and tireless work ethic. On Thursday March 4, 2004, after five weeks on a newly prescribed anti-depressant medication, Tooker Gomberg jumped from the MacDonald Bridge into the Halifax harbor. His bicycle, helmet and suicide note were found on the bridge. Family and friends have charged that Gomberg had a negative response to the medication, which pushed him deeper into an abyss that could have been avoided. "Take the Tooker" is a memorial initiative to create an extensive bikeway, to be named after Gomberg, in the city of Toronto. His partner, Angela Bischoff, continues to organize around issues of mental health and the pharmaceutical industry, as well as continuing the anti-nuclear and ecological sustainability work she and Gomberg shared.

Jesse Purcell

Albert "Ginger" Goodwin

"In order to throw this system over we have got to organize as a class and fight them as class against class."

A SLIGHT, RED-HAIRED, English coal miner named Albert Goodwin immigrated to Canada at age 19. Goodwin, a union activist, orator and soccer enthusiast, worked in coal mines in Cape Breton before moving west to British Colombia, and was soon elected vice president of the British Columbia Federation of Labour. He made a name for himself as a gifted union organizer, advocating for the eight-hour workday and fair wages in an industry that historically provided its workers with contemptible conditions at best. In 1916, Goodwin ran unsuccessfully for office on the Socialist Party ticket in Trail, British Columbia.

In 1917, during the First World War, "Ginger" Goodwin led a month long strike in British Colombia at the world's largest smelter, the Consolidated Mining and Smelting Company, demanding an eight-hour workday. Prior to orchestrating the strike, Goodwin had failed a medical examination for the Canadian Army's war draft, likely due to the condition of his lungs from a life of mining coal. During the strike however, he was called back for reevaluation and suspiciously declared fit for overseas service. After an unsuccessful appeal, Goodwin fled underground. He managed to live for several months in the woods near Cumberland, BC, with the help of locals and friends in the mining union. Goodwin was eventually discovered and murdered by a hired constable who never faced formal charges. In 1918, the occasion of Albert "Ginger" Goodwin's funeral in Vancouver sparked the first general strike in Canadian history.

"WE ABOLITIONWOMEN ARE TURNING THE WORLD UPSIDE DOWN" - ANGELINA

Angelina & Sarah Grimké

{February 20, 1805 - October 26, 1879} Angelina
{November 26, 1792 - December 23, 1873} Sarah

"If persecution is the means which God has ordained for the accomplishment of this great end, EMANCIPATION, then, in dependence upon Him for strength to bear it, I feel as if I could say, let it come; for it is my deep, solemn, deliberate conviction that this is a cause worth dying for." -Angelina Grimké

SARAH AND ANGELINA GRIMKÉ were sisters born into a wealthy, slaveholding plantation family in Charleston, South Carolina. Disgusted by the cruelty of slavery, and thwarted by both their family and church in their efforts to educate slaves, both women moved north to Philadelphia. There, they joined the Religious Society of Friends (Quakers) and became the first women to join the American Anti-Slavery Society. With the younger Angelina being a powerful orator, the pair travelled around New England inciting people to take political action against slavery and encouraging the rights of women to engage in such discourse and activism.

Sarah's strength as a writer led to her creation of the first Biblically-based argument for the emancipation of women that took into account class and skin color. Through their lectures and writings, the Grimké sisters fought for the abolition of slavery in the South and the necessity of ending racial prejudice in the North, calling for an end to northern business collaborations with southern slave owners. They argued for true equality regardless of skin color and asserted that women were responsible and moral human beings who have the right and obligation to act dutifully in their society and thus to engage in the political sphere. Their actions were remarkable in the antebellum era, as their fiery tracts and speeches called for a radical abolitionism that even the Quakers often found uncomfortable, all at a time when women were rarely seen speaking publicly to crowds.

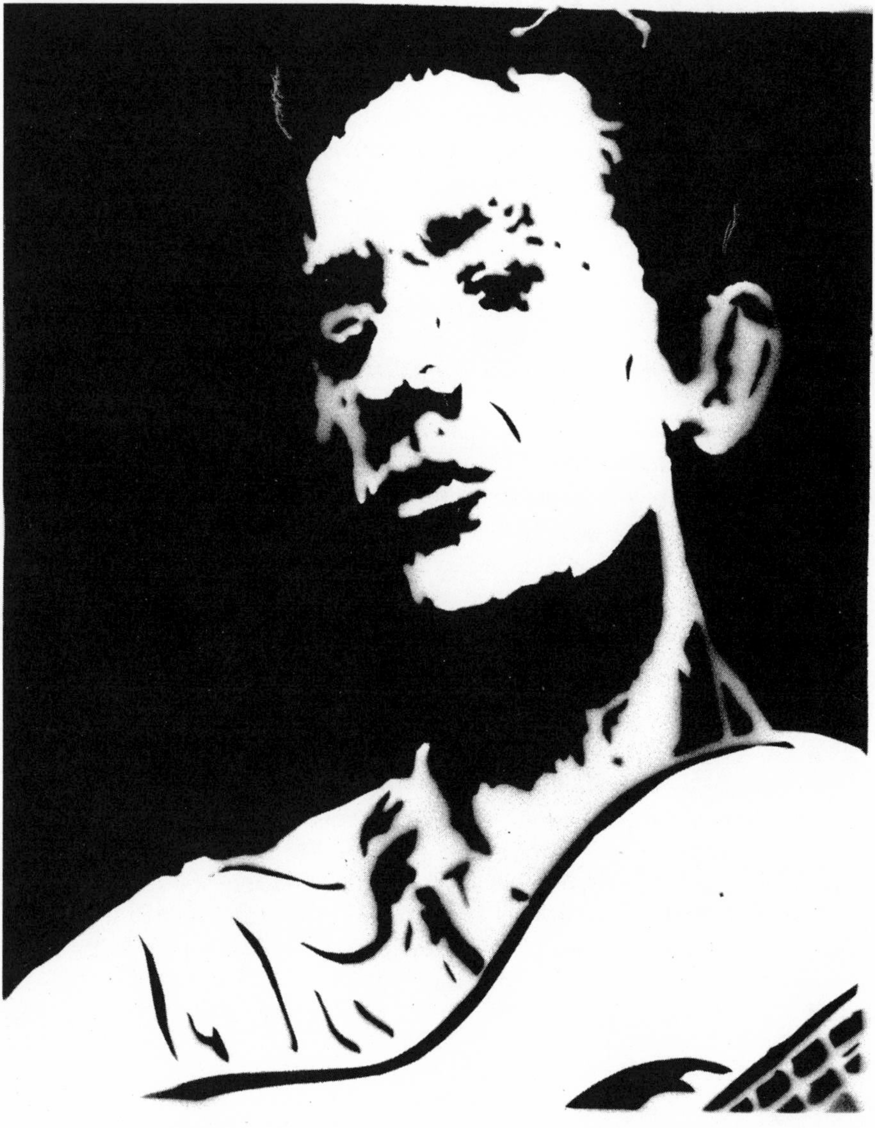

Chris Stain

Woody Guthrie

"The note of hope is the only note that can help us or save us from falling to the bottom of the heap of evolution, because largely, about all a human being is anyway, is just a hoping machine, and any song that says, the pleasures I have seen in all of my trouble, are the things I never can get—don't worry—the human race will sing this way as long as there is a human race."

WOODROW WILSON GUTHRIE WAS born in Okemah, Oklahoma, a place he called "one of the singingest, square-dancingest, drinkingest, yellingest, fist-fightingest, shootingest, razor-carryingest of ranch and farm towns which blossomed into an oil boom town." He became widely known for his original, accessible folk songs that often told the plight of working people and their families in Depression-era United States and beyond. While Guthrie performed live on the radio for many years, his first recordings were made in the 1940s by the folk historian Alan Lomax, who likewise encouraged Guthrie to pen his memoir *Bound for Glory*. Guthrie was friendly with the communist movement in the U.S. and although he was never formally a member of any explicitly communist organizations, he maintained a virulent anti-fascist stance in his work.

Woody Guthrie worked alongside and inspired such folk greats as Pete Seeger, Leadbelly, Bob Dylan, and Bruce Springsteen. He wrote hundreds of songs on subjects ranging from the Dust Bowl to child rearing, from train-hopping to the trial of Sacco and Vanzetti. Truncated versions of his song "This Land Is Your Land," originally a critique of working class plight and private property, are taught in classrooms across the United States as a standard accompaniment to the "Star-Spangled Banner," although these versions typically leave out the verse in which Guthrie suggests that the people should instead follow the directions on the reverse side of the "No Trespassing" sign, where "it didn't say nothin'."

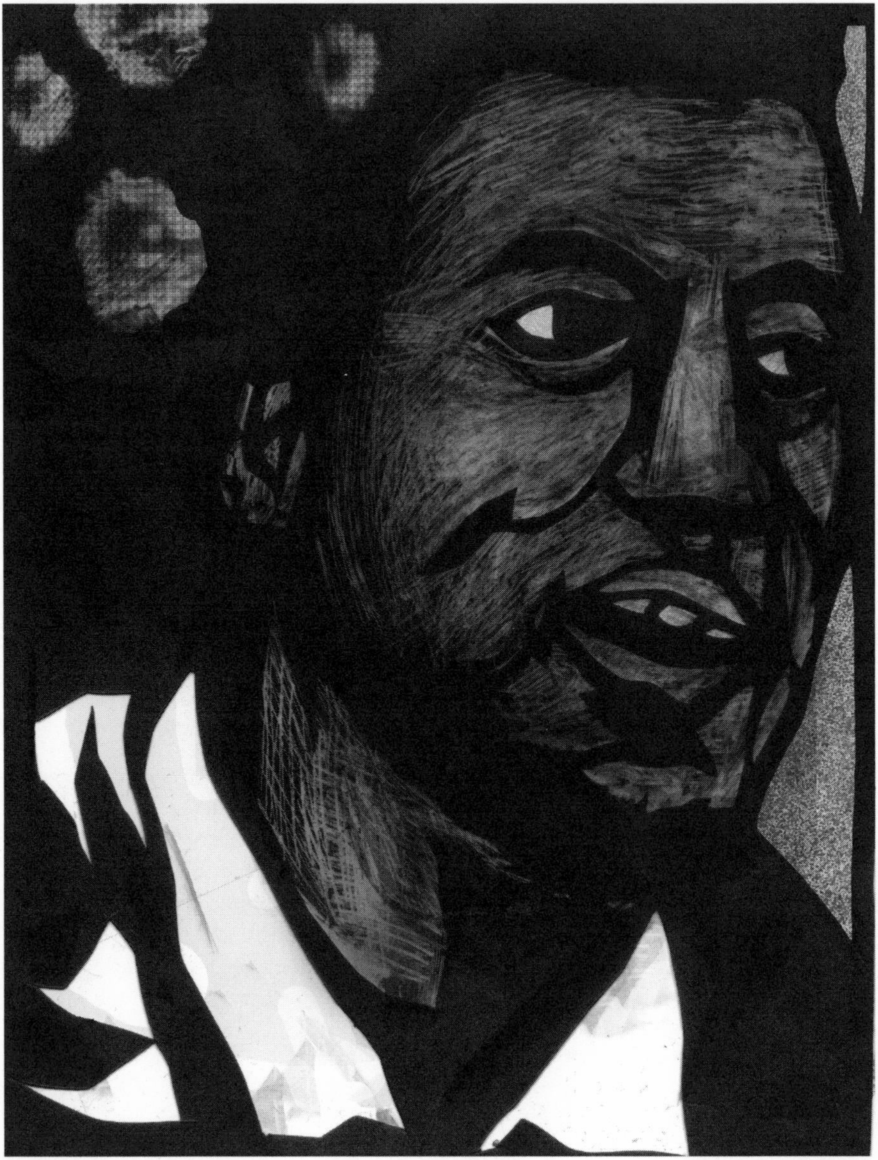

Erik Ruin

Fred Hampton

"A lot of people get the word revolution mixed up and they think revolution's a bad word. Revolution is nothing but like having a sore on your body and then you put something on that sore to cure that infection. And I'm telling you that we're living in an infectious society right now. I'm telling you that we're living in a sick society. And anybody that endorses integrating into this sick society before it's cleaned up is a man who's committing a crime against the people."

FRED HAMPTON WAS BORN in Chicago, raised in the suburbs and introduced to activism as a youth organizer with the National Association for the Advancement of Colored People (NAACP). He joined the Black Panther Party in 1969 and quickly rose through the ranks, being recognized as a compelling speaker and an effective organizer. At the time of his death at 22, he was chairman of the Illinois chapter of the Black Panther Party and was expected to be named to the Party's Central Committee's Chief of Staff.

Hampton was adept at building alliances amongst like-minded groups; he and other Chicago Black Panther members brokered a non-aggression pact among the most powerful street gangs in the city. He coined the term "rainbow coalition" to describe the multi-racial alliance they were building. His effectiveness brought him to the attention of the FBI, who engineered splits within the groups and hired an informant to infiltrate the Panthers as part of their Counter-Intelligence Program (COINTELPRO) against "subversive" organizations in the U.S.

On the morning of December 4, 1969, a task force from the Cook County State Attorney's Office raided his apartment and killed Hampton in his sleep in a barrage of gunfire, along with fellow Panther Mark Clark. His son, Fred Hampton Jr., in utero when his father was killed, continues on his father's work as an activist, currently serving as president and chair of the Prisoners of Conscience Committee.

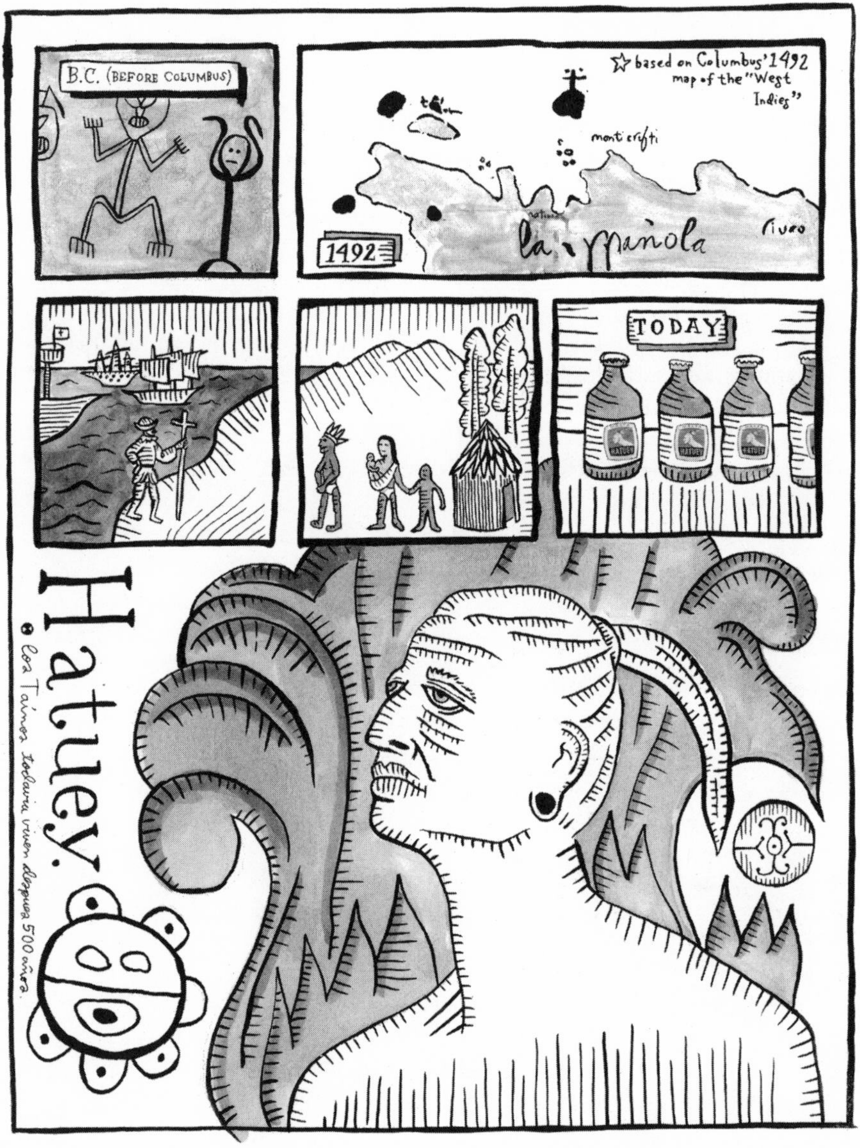
B.C. (BEFORE COLUMBUS)
☆ based on Columbus' 1492 map of the "West Indies"
monti crifti
la ispañola
rivero
1492
TODAY
Hatuey.
los Taínos todavía viven después 500 años.

Hatuey

"They tell us, these tyrants, that they adore a God of peace and equality, and yet they usurp our land and make us their slaves. They speak to us of an immortal soul and of their eternal rewards and punishments, and yet they rob our belongings, seduce our women, violate our daughters." -Terence Cannon

HATUEY WAS AN ESTEEMED Taíno Cacique (leader) and freedom fighter who fought against Spanish colonial forces in the New World. In the early 16th century, he led the struggle against Catholicism and is since celebrated as Cuba's first national hero. His anti-colonial leadership is only predated by the activities of Anacoana, an important female Cacique who was hanged for treason in 1504.

Born on the island of Qusqueya (present-day Haiti and Dominican Republic), Hatuey escaped Spanish control by traveling to Cuba. In Cuba, he hoped to organize the local population to resist Spanish rule. Using guerrilla tactics centuries before Che Guevara successfully employed them, Hatuey organized his forces into small *focos* (small, swift paramilitary groups) that carried out surprise attacks on the colonizers. Known for his steadfast bravery in face of Spanish violence, Hatuey was captured and sentenced to be burned at the cross in February 1512. While awaiting execution, a Catholic priest attempted to convert Hatuey to Christianity. When told that he would go to heaven if converted, he responded that he would rather be in hell with the murderous Christians so that he could continue to fight against them.

Nearly 500 years after his death, Hatuey's anti-colonial fortitude remains an important symbol of Indigenous and anti-capitalist struggles throughout Latin America and the world. Sadly, his likeness is more widely known for being the namesake of various consumer products, including both a beer and a soda, than it is for his important role in fighting colonialism.

INDUSTRIAL UNIONISM

ABOLITION OF THE WAGE SYSTEM

IWW

ONE BIG UNION OF ALL THE WORKERS

THE GREATEST THING ON EARTH

Sabotage means to push back, pull out or break off the fangs of Capitalism
W.D. Haywood

Big Bill Haywood

{FEBRUARY 4, 1869 - MAY 18, 1928}

"Sabotage means to push back, pull out or break off the fangs of Capitalism."

WILLIAM "BIG BILL" HAYWOOD was a bear of a man with a gentle demeanor who stood up for working class people worldwide. Born in Salt Lake City, Utah, in 1869, as a young man he worked in the mines of Nevada and received little formal education. By 1902 he was the secretary-treasurer of the Western Federation of Miners union, and had developed a radical analysis of working class struggles. He would eventually become an important leader in the movement to unionize industrial workers with revolution in mind.

In Chicago, in 1905, Haywood helped found the Industrial Workers of the World (IWW). The IWW was conceived as "One Big Union" of workers, which would differ from the more easily marginalized craft-based unions of the past, where workers were organized by skill or industry. Challenging the racism, sexism, and nationalism of existing unions, the founders of the IWW meant to create a radical organization that would demonstrate a clear counter-power to the ruling class through direct action and working class solidarity across trades. Members were known colloquially as "Wobblies" and their new union provided a radical opposition to capitalism in the U.S..

Haywood was a militant socialist, and endorsed the "general strike" and sabotage as tools to challenge oppressive management, with the ultimate goal of overthrowing capitalism and eliminating the wage labor system. He became one of the principal strike leaders and speakers for the IWW, and helped coordinate the Lawrence Textile Strike (1912) and the silk workers strike in Paterson, New Jersey (1913). In 1918, he was sentenced to twenty years in prison under the Sedition Act as part of a nationwide government crackdown on the IWW and war resisters. He jumped bail in 1921 and fled to Russia, where he died in 1928.

In a revolution, when the ceaseless slow accumulation of centuries bursts into volcanic eruption, the meteoric flares and flights above are a meaningless chaos and lend themselves to infinite caprice and romanticism unless the observer sees them always as projections of the sub-soil from which they came. The writer has sought not only to analyse, but to demonstrate in their movement, the economic forces of the age; their moulding of society and politics, of men in the mass and individual men; the powerful reaction of these on their environment at one of those rare moments when society is at boiling point and therefore fluid.

· Toussaint · L'Ouverture ·

· Sir · Frank · Worrell ·

CLR James

Dylan Miner

C. L. R. James

CYRIL LIONEL ROBERT JAMES, better known simply as C.L.R., was a black radical intellectual born in Trinidad when the island was still a British colony. James was active in the Beacon Group, an anti-colonial organization in Trinidad, while also working as a schoolteacher. Relocating to England in the early 1930s, he began to advocate for the liberation of the West Indies and became involved in the International African Service Bureau, a socialist Pan-African organization.

Unlike many leftist intellectuals, James was very interested in sports and worked for some time as a cricket journalist. His book, *Beyond a Boundary,* has become a classic in its complex analysis of sports from a Marxist perspective. In 1937, a few years after arriving in England, James published *World Revolution*, a history of the Communist International. Although in many ways a Trotskyite, James was a nonconformist in his Marxist thinking.

In the late 1930s, James traveled to the United States, where alongside Raya Dunayevskaya and Grace Lee Boggs, he founded the Johnson-Forest Tendency, which proposed a new, fundamentalist inclination of Marxist thought that rejected most existing socialist governments as being state capitalist. A prolific author, James' role as both an anti-capitalist intellectual and anti-colonial activist remains influential through his numerous works and contributions to theory. He eventually left the U.S. after being threatened with deportation for overstaying his visa by a decade.

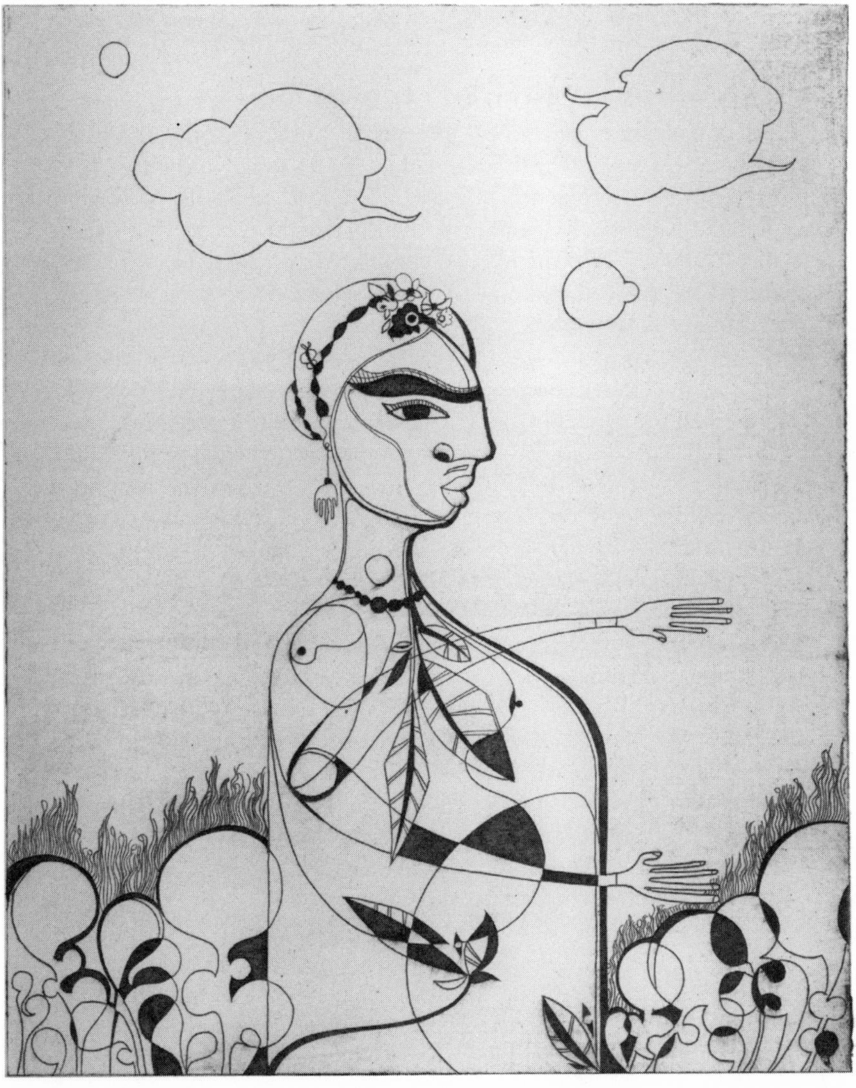

Favianna Rodriguez

Frida Kahlo

"They thought I was a Surrealist, but I wasn't. I never painted dreams.
I painted my own reality."

HER PAINTINGS, IT HAS been said, are the living biography of Frida Kahlo; it is otherwise nearly impossible to separate the artist's life from her work. Born in Mexico as it was about to erupt in a revolution, Kahlo, a childhood polio survivor, was a young intellectual but a distracted student who often skipped class and fell in with a socialist-nationalist group of students in high school. Plans to pursue medical studies after her graduation were violently sidetracked when, at age 18, a bus she was riding in was crushed by a streetcar. Kahlo received multiple near-lethal injuries, including a punctured womb, which would require dozens of surgeries and keep her in pain for much of the rest of her life.

Frida Kahlo had never meant to take painting seriously, but the streetcar crash left her bedridden for over a year. Borrowing her father's paints and brushes and working from a makeshift easel, Kahlo began to create paintings that would far outlast her relatively short life. In 1929 she married Diego Rivera, an established social realist painter 20 years her elder, with whom she would forever be associated. Throughout their tumultuous relationship, the two were associated with the Communists, even housing Leon Trotsky for a time after he fled from Stalinist Russia.

Kahlo's work illustrated her personal struggle through esoteric imagery, blended with a palette of stylized traditional pre-Columbian and Mexican pop imagery. Her paintings, viewed alongside her openly bisexual and poly-amorous life, have helped to dismantle and re-imagine gender assumptions and the acceptable "norms" of beauty.

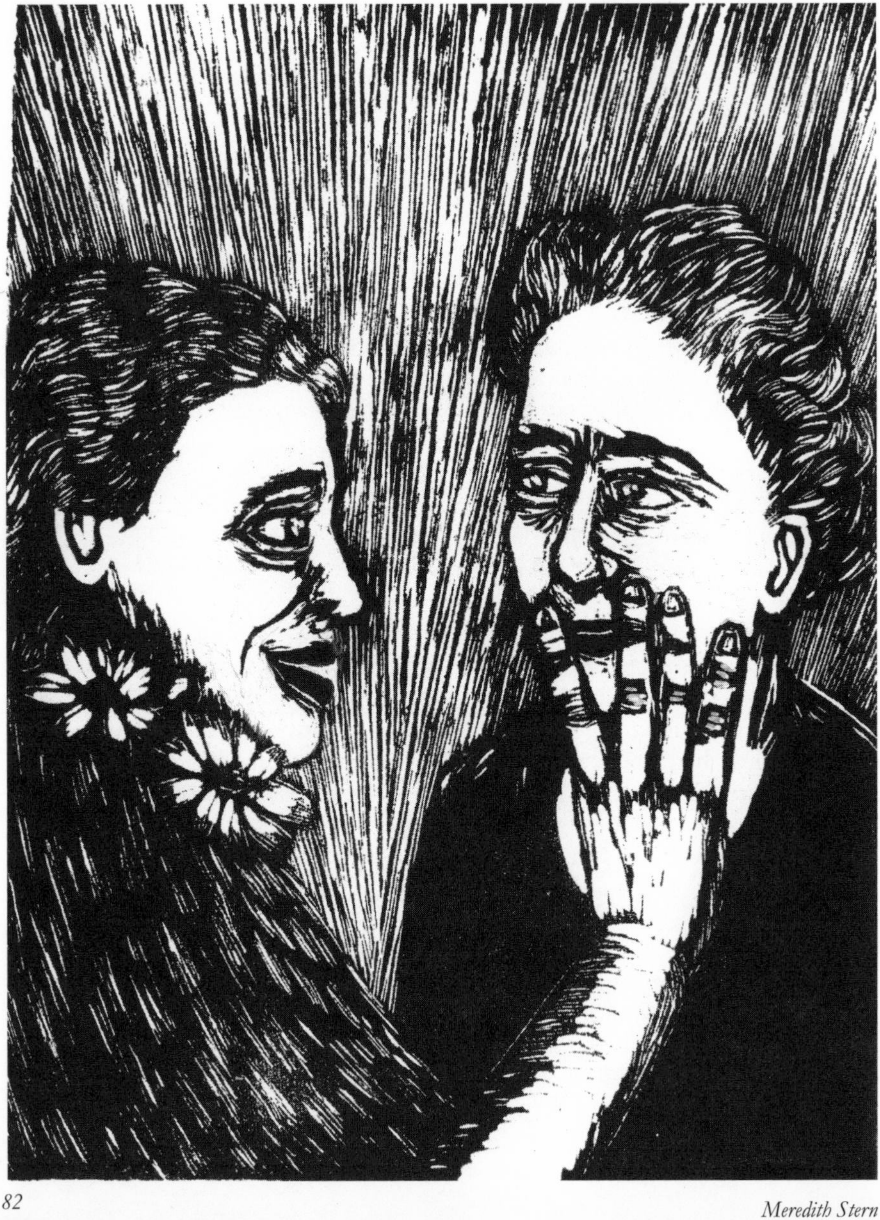

Meredith Stern

Helen Keller

"Until the spirit of love for our fellowmen, regardless of race, color, or creed, shall fill the world, making real in our lives and our deeds the actuality of human brotherhood—until the great mass of the people shall be filled with the sense of responsibility for each other's welfare, social justice can never be attained."

BORN IN TUSCUMBIA, ALABAMA, Helen Keller had lost her sight and hearing, the result of illness, at only 19 months old. At the age of six, Keller met Anne Sullivan, an innovative instructor who taught her how to use language and who would remain her companion and teacher for most of Keller's life. Keller would go on to be a unique and compelling character, sentimentalized through her struggles with her disability yet controversial in her political views.

Helen Keller's social activism and writing is often downplayed, and her unique challenges with language often serve as her sole identity in popular tales. However, the poverty of the working class deeply troubled Keller. She joined the Socialist Party in 1909 and wrote for Industrial Workers of the World (IWW) publications. She was among the many women who led international peace efforts during World War I, and helped found the American Civil Liberties Union (ACLU) in 1920. An outspoken advocate of civil rights, Keller campaigned for women's suffrage and birth control education. Her sharp intellect, sincerity and passion inspired global adoration of her writing and lectures, and her charming personality led to a role as an informal international ambassador.

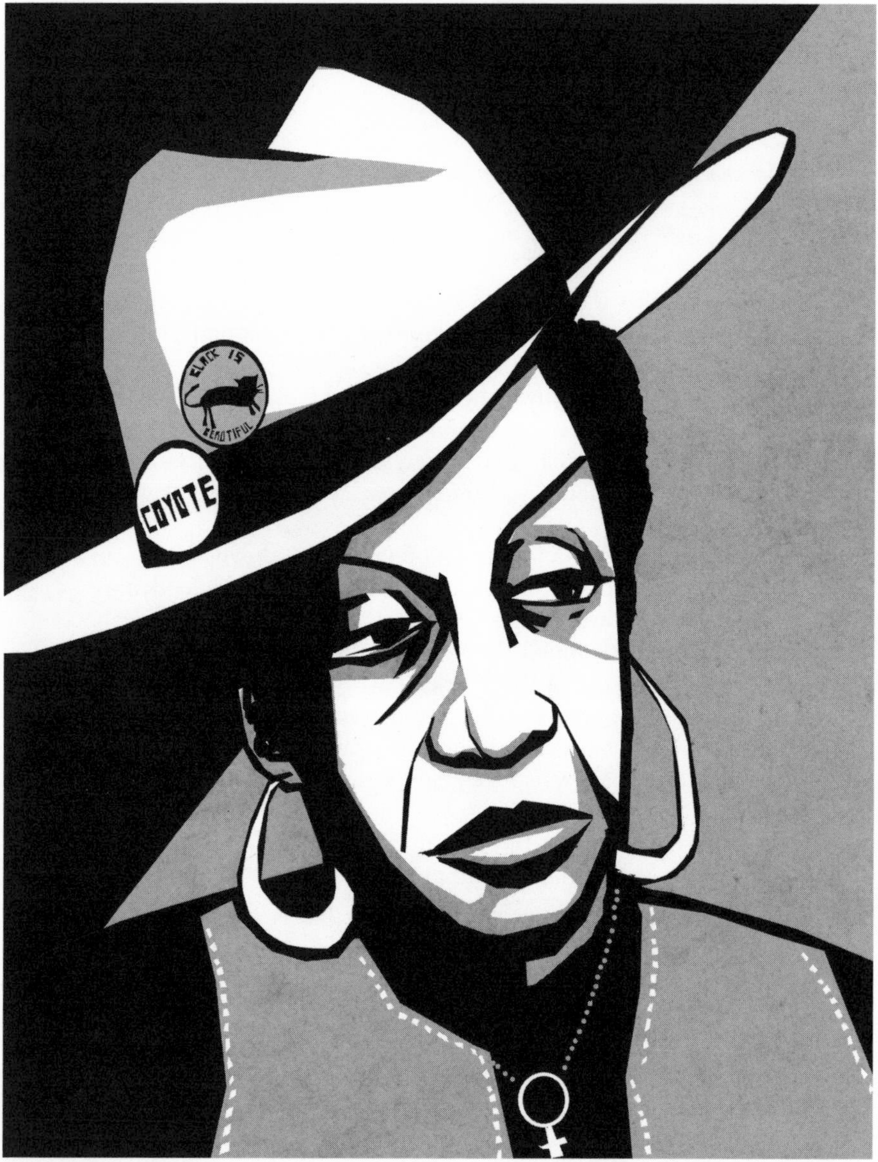
BLACK IS
BEAUTIFUL
COYOTE

Alec "Icky" Dunn

Florynce Kennedy

"I'm just a loud-mouthed middle-aged colored lady with a fused spine and three feet of intestines missing and a lot of people think I'm crazy. Maybe you do too, but I never stop to wonder why I'm not like other people. The mystery to me is why more people aren't like me."

FLORYNCE KENNEDY WAS BORN and raised in a working class black family in Kansas City, Missouri. She followed her sister to New York City in 1942 and began law school at Columbia (after being denied admission and threatening a lawsuit) in 1948. Three years later, she had her own law office, and eventually she became known for representing Billie Holiday and Charlie Parker in lawsuits against their record companies. A charismatic speaker and writer, she became increasingly politicized and well-known in the 1960s and 70s for her strident support of liberation struggles, feminism, sex-worker rights and abortion.

Humorous, stylish, highly critical and engaged in the moment, Florynce Kennedy challenged the way feminists, black women and activists had to behave and look. She was an activist in the court as well as on the streets. Dubbed "radicalism's rudest mouth," she led a mass "pee-in" at Harvard to protest the lack of free toilets, consistently organized against racist and sexist media and advertising, and was an early supporter of COYOTE (Call Off Your Old Tired Ethics, a sex workers' union). Her personal flair and sense of theater made her a breath of fresh air in the increasingly "hard" politics of the 1970s.

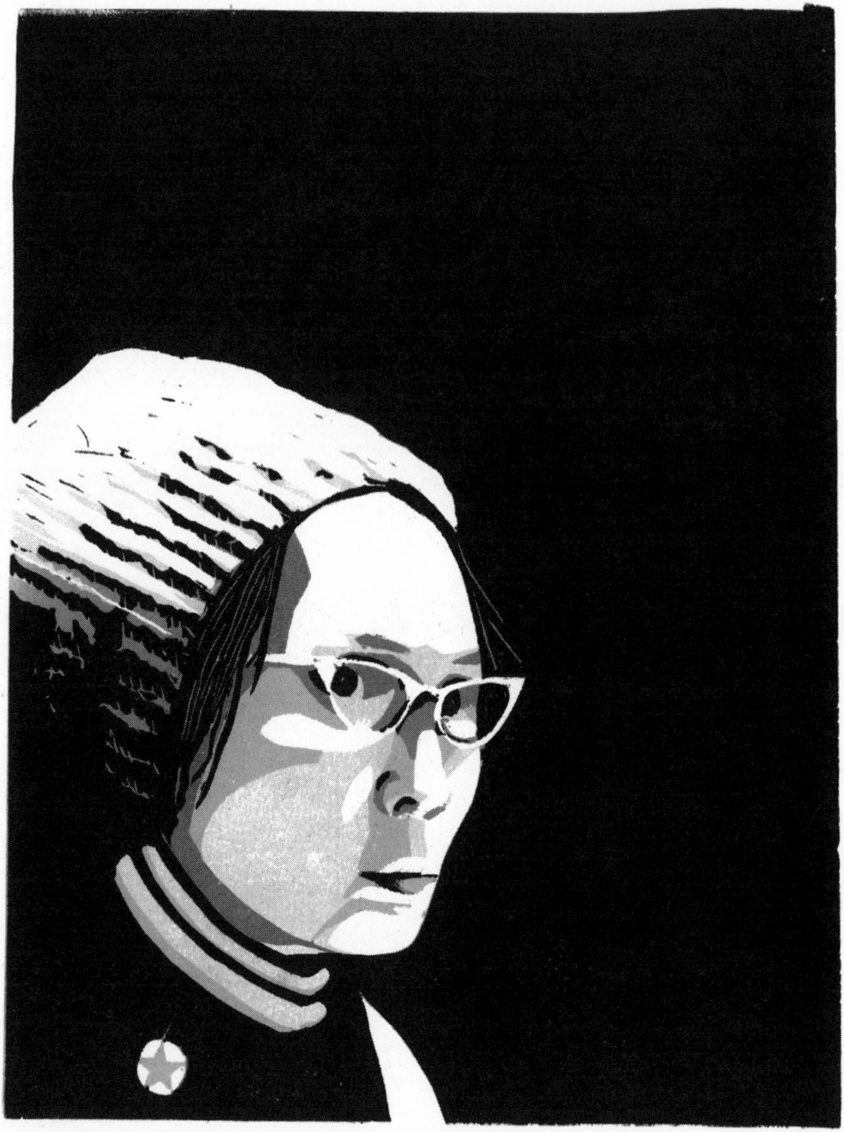

Alec "Icky" Dunn

Yuri Kochiyama

"The Movement is contagious and awesome because the people in it are the spirit of the Movement. And the Movement will continue because new concerned people will rejuvenate and revitalize this never-ending struggle. It just always makes you want to be part of it."

YURI KOCHIYAMA WAS BORN Mary Nakahara, a first-generation Japanese emigrant born and raised in San Pedro, California. Following the Japanese attack on Pearl Harbor in 1941, her family was swept up in a nationwide forced relocation of people of Japanese ancestry to internment camps. In the lead up to U.S. involvement in World War II, over 100,000 Japanese were imprisoned in such camps, even though well over half of them were legal U.S. citizens. Kochiyama lived for three years in an internment camp in Arkansas, where she met her husband, Bill Kochiyama. The two eventually relocated to public housing in Harlem, New York.

A mother of six, Kochiyama became a dedicated organizer in liberation struggles in the African-American and Asian-American communities. Kochiyama and her husband joined the Harlem Parents Committee, challenging the city to improve traffic conditions in areas where children were often hit by cars, as well as taking on issues of education in the school district. The pair enrolled three of their children in the Harlem Freedom School, an effort to work across community borders of ethnicity. Yuri Kochiyama was heavily influenced by Malcolm X, whom she befriended in the final years of his life, and was present when he was assassinated in February of 1965. In 1977, Kochiyama and several members of the Young Lords Party occupied the Statue of Liberty to draw attention to five Puerto Rican political prisoners and their country's independence movement. Kochiyama continues to be heavily involved in global liberation struggles and political prisoner support.

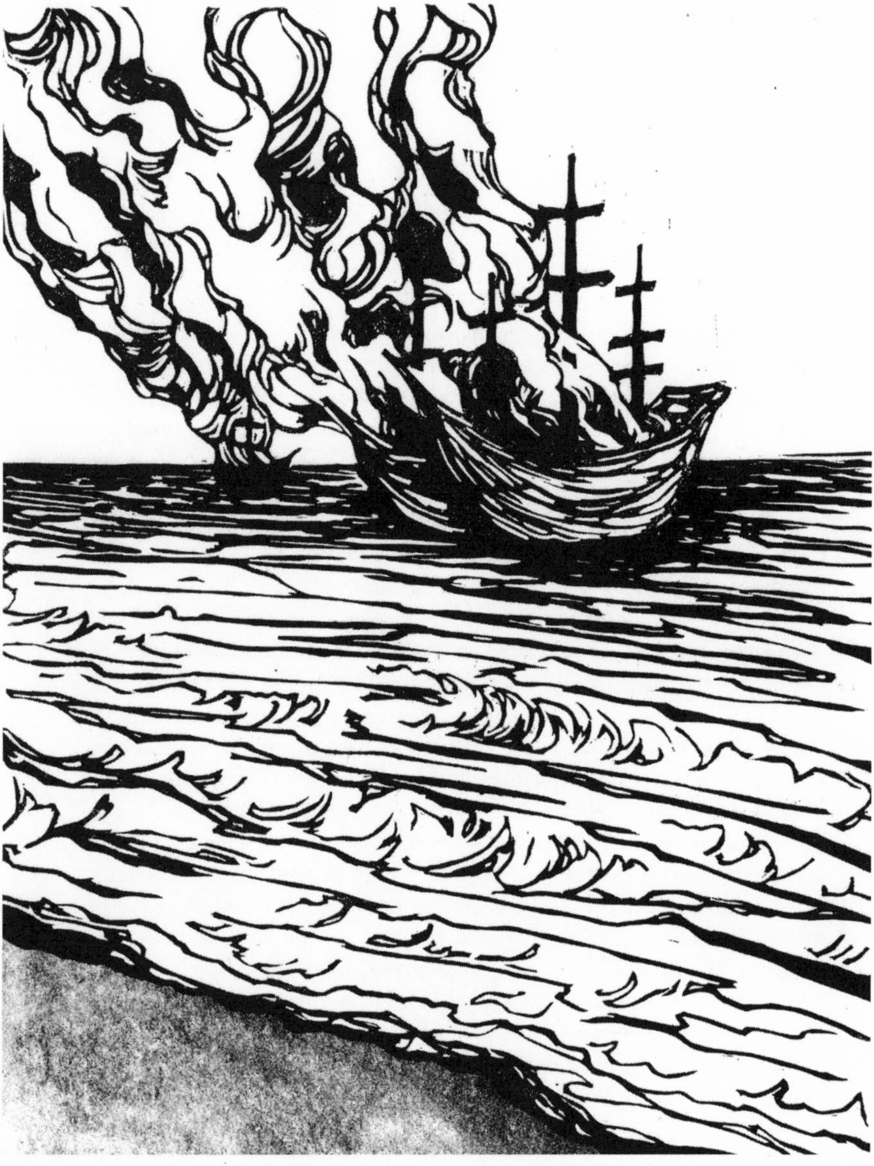

Pete Yahnke

Toussaint L'Ouverture

{MAY 20, 1743 - APRIL 7TH, 1803}

"I was born a slave, but nature gave me a soul of a free man."

TOUSSANINT L'OUVERTURE WAS A former slave and self-educated, literate Haitian who went on to become a leading general in the Haitian Revolution, considered by many to be the only victorious slave revolt in history because it alone resulted in the formation of a new country led by people of African descent. In this light, L'Ouverture is credited with declaring the end of slavery 61 years before Abraham Lincoln would do so in the United States. He also drafted and implemented the first constitution for Haiti, the second ever authored for a republic in the western hemisphere, which forced European nations to seriously consider the aspirations of colonized black populations.

As a military leader, L'Ouverture was responsible for deflecting the armies of England and Spain in brutal skirmishes on behalf of the French. After repelling other European colonial forces however, L'Ouverture declared himself governor-for-life and sought to rule Haiti (then known as Saint-Domingue) as an autonomous state. Three weeks following a treaty with France, he was captured by renewed French armies, governed by Napoleon Bonaparte, and transported to Fort de Joux prison in France where he died of pneumonia. The war for Haitian independence would continue, with the French finally withdrawing the following year. The success of L'Ouverture's audacious leadership has served as inspiration for hundreds of slave insurrections.

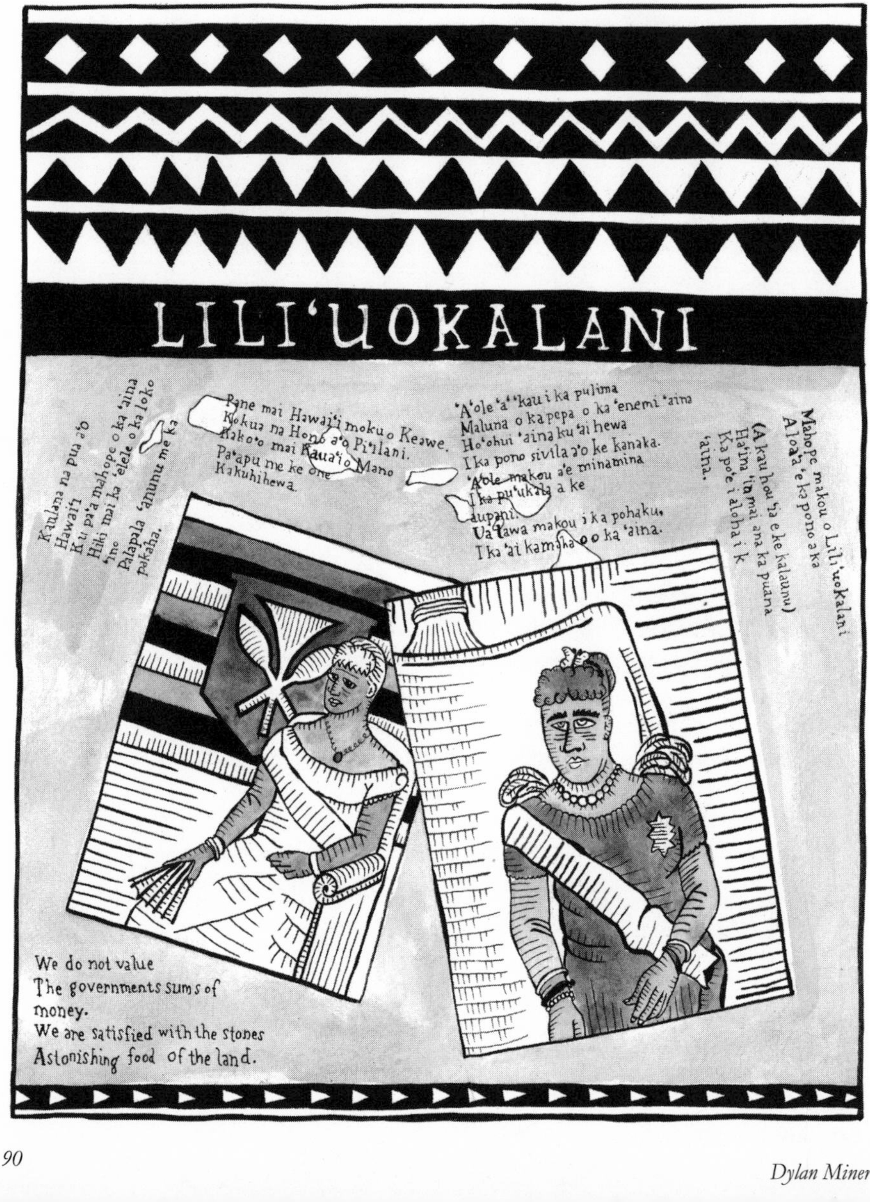
LILI'UOKALANI
Kaulana na pua a'o
Hawai'i
Ku pa'a mahope o ka 'aina
Hiki mai ka 'elele o ka loko
'ino
Palapala 'anunu me ka
pakaha.
Pane mai Hawai'i moku o Keawe.
Kokua na Hono a'o Pi'ilani.
Kako'o mai Kaua'i o Mano
Pa'apu me ke one
Kakuhihewa.
'A'ole 'a'e kau i ka pulima
Maluna o ka pepa o ka 'enemi 'aina
Ho'ohui 'aina ku'ai hewa
I ka pono sivila a'o ke kanaka.
'A'ole makou a'e minamina
I ka pu'ukala a ke
aupuni.
Ua lawa makou i ka pohaku,
I ka 'ai kamaha'o o ka 'aina.
Mahope makou o Lili'uokalani
A loa'a 'e ka pono a ka
'aina.
(A kau hou 'ia e ke kalaunu)
Ha'ina 'ia mai ana ka puana
Ka po'e i aloha i k
We do not value
The governments sums of
money.
We are satisfied with the stones
Astonishing food of the land.

Lili'uokalani

LILI'UOKALANI WAS THE LAST *kānaka maoli* (indigenous monarch) of the sovereign Ke Aupuni O Hawai'i (Kingdom of Hawai'i). Born Lydia Lili'u Loloku Walania Wewehi Kamaka'eha to Analea Keohokalole and Caesar Kaluaiku Kapa'akea, she was adopted by Abner Pākī and his wife Laura Kōnia following *maoli* protocol. In 1877, Lili'uokalani became the heir to the Hawaiian throne, following a complex family struggle over the dominion of Ke Aupuni O Hawai'i. She preceded her brother Kalākaua to the throne in 1891. As monarch, one of the first moves she made was to re-write the constitution in order to restore power to the Kingdom's *maoli* (native Hawaiian citizenry). Threatened by this attempt and other changes in the islands, settler businessmen sought annexation to the United States.

In January 1893, Lili'uokalani was dethroned by a group of U.S. and European capitalists and missionaries known as the Citizen's Committee of Public Safety. Armed U.S. forces easily entered the island. An illegitimate Provisional Government was established until the Republic of Hawai'i was created, with Sanford Dole, cousin of pineapple plantation magnate James Dole, as its president. Today, *maoli* activists continue to struggle to restore Indigenous control of Ke Aupuni O Hawai'i. "Kaulana Nā Pua," a song written after the 1893 coup d'etat, speaks to the continued struggles of the Hawaiian people:

'A'ole mākou a'e minamina	We do not value
I ka pu'ukālā a ke aupuni	The government's hills of money
Ua lawa mākou i ka pōhaku	We are satisfied with the rocks
I ka 'ai kamaha'o o ka'āina	The wondrous food of the land
Mahope mākou o Lili'ulani	We support Lili'uokalani
A loa'a e ka pono o ka'āina	Who has won the rights of the land
Ha'ina 'ia mai ana ka puana	The story is told
Ka po'e i aloha i ka 'āina	Of the people who love the land.

"THE POWER of our unexpressed or unrecognized feeling... in order to perpetuate itself, every oppression must corrupt or distort those various sources of power within the culture of the oppressed that can provide energy for change. For women this has meant a suppression of the erotic as a considered source of power and information within our lives."

92

Mary Tremonte

Audre Lorde

{FEBRUARY 18, 1934 - NOVEMBER 17, 1992}

AUDRE LORDE, BORN AUDREY, grew up in New York City to Grenadian immigrant parents. So nearsighted as to be nearly blind, Lorde didn't learn to speak until learning to read at the age of four. She started dropping the "y" in Audrey as a child, liking the even look of "AUDRELORDE." The empowerment of this self-naming would be an important theme in her later work. While still in high school, her first poem was published in *Seventeen Magazine*. She worked for years as a teen librarian in the New York Public Library system, making a particular effort to include more black voices on the shelves.

Lorde's essays, novels and poems explicitly explore connections among myriad forms of oppression. She charged that the feminist movement held the experiences of white, middle-class women as normative, and controversially advocated for a movement inclusive of individual experiences in class, race, age and health. A writer who saw herself in relational dialogue with the rest of the world, Lorde explained that her work owed much to her ancestors, to the love and support of women, and to African and African-American artists. She insisted in her poetry and prose that without community and coalition across differences there would be no true liberation from oppression. Lorde's visibility as a black lesbian feminist poet was a very deliberate choice, a concerted effort to battle isolation amongst people who are often marginalized or made invisible in American society, and to them say: "We are not alone."

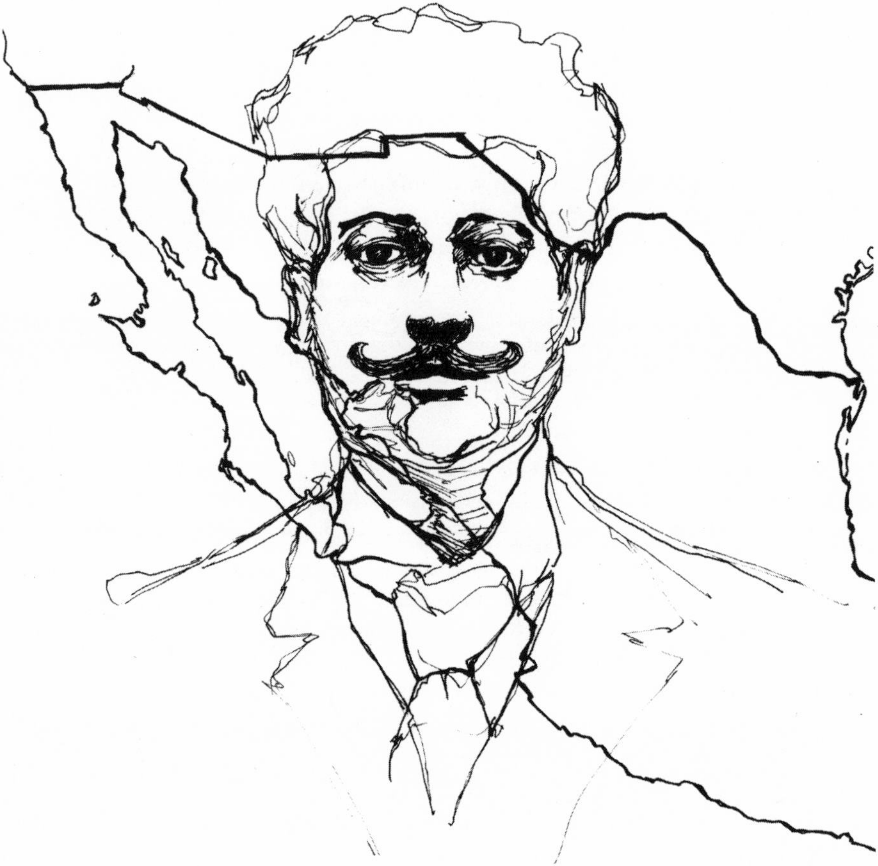

Pete Yahnke

Ricardo Flores Magón

"Anarchism aspires to establish peace forever among all the races of the earth by suppressing the source of all evil: the right of private property. If this is not a beautiful ideal, what is?"

RICARDO FLORES MAGÓN WAS a Mexican writer and anarchist theorist who played an influential role in the development of the Mexican Revolution. As a journalist, Magón published several revolutionary newspapers, although *Regeneración*, which he started with his brother Jesus, would be the first to land him in jail in 1900. Arrested again in 1904 for more anti-government publishing activity, Magón fled north to San Diego, St. Louis and eventually west to Los Angeles. Drawing from his readings while in prison, Magón began to form an anarchist analysis of power in the Americas. Not a Mexican nationalist, he sought cooperation between the Mexican and U.S. working class, calling for a revolutionary inter-regionalist approach to wage and labor issues.

Magón did much of his organizing and publishing with his brother Enrique, and together the brothers were successful in restarting *Regeneración* from their exile in the U.S. and developing a clandestine network of distribution throughout highly-illiterate, rural Mexico. The two brothers founded the Mexican Liberal Party (Partido Liberal Mexicano) in 1906. In direct opposition to the presidency of Porfirio Diaz, the PLM attempted revolts in 1906, 1908, and finally with some success in 1911 when the small, underfunded anarchist army seized several cities in the Baja Peninsula. Repeatedly arrested for these and other activities during the Mexican Revolution, Magón died in Leavenworth Penitentiary in Kansas from unknown causes. There has been speculation that prison officials neglected his declining health.

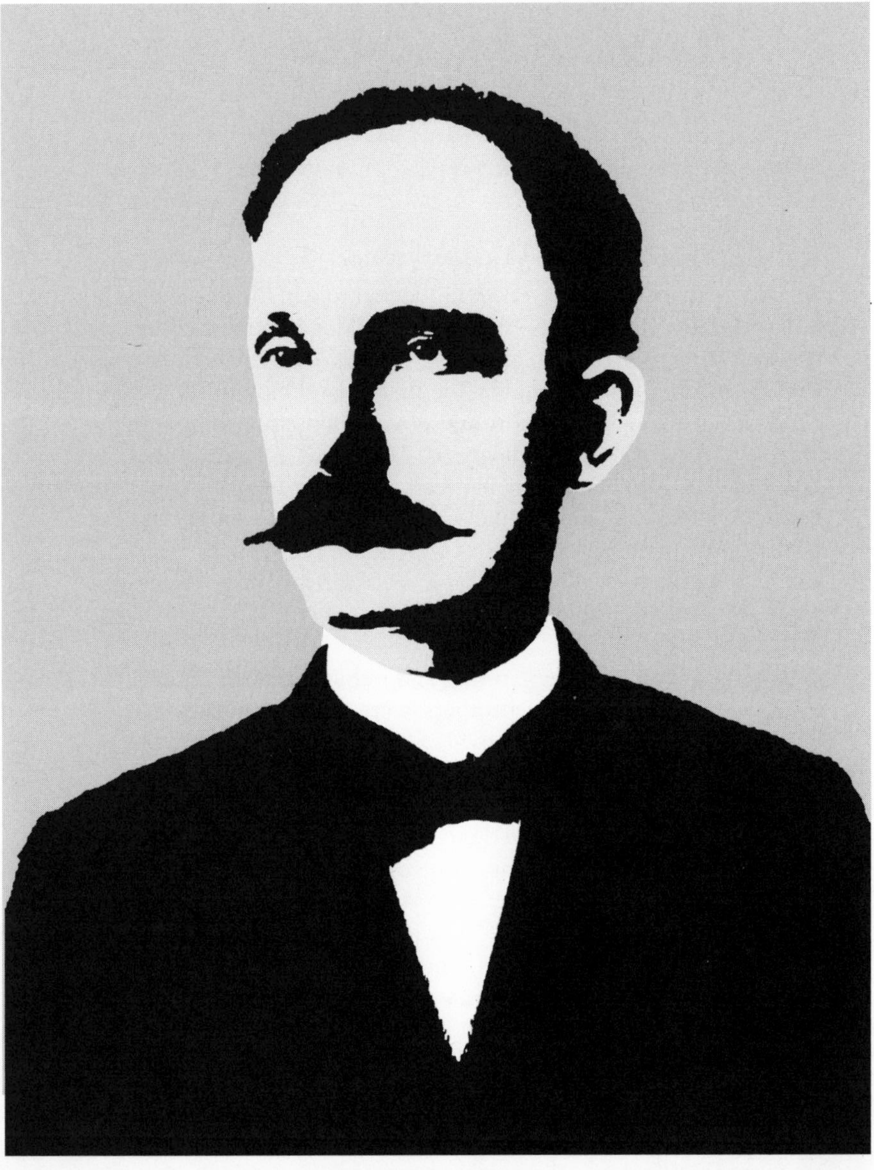

Jesus Barraza

"It is necessary to make virtue fashionable."

{JANUARY 28, 1853 - MAY 19, 1895}

JOSÉ JULIÁN MARTÍ PÉREZ was a Cuban nationalist poet, revolutionary philosopher and political theorist. His role in organizing Cuban forces in the successful third war against Spanish colonial rule was significant and the victory helped deter subsequent expansionism by the United States. Martí's vision was of a democratic, self-ruled Cuba, free from colonialism, and he hoped to unite Cubans across class and race boundaries to achieve this goal. His prescient thoughts and writings on future U.S. interest in Cuba are of continual influence today.

At the age of 16, Martí was imprisoned for seditious writings that addressed his hopes for the collapse of Spanish rule over his homeland. He was transferred to Spain and eventually released, allowing him to continue to write and publish his beliefs. Although Martí was devoted to Cuba, he spent much of his time away from the country, bouncing in continual exile across the Atlantic before ending up in the U.S., where he toured the country garnering support for Cuban liberation. After a failed attempt to sail three ships, carrying the supplies needed to confront the Spanish, to Cuba, Martí and others finally arrived in 1895 to begin what would become the Cuban War of Independence. He was killed in an early skirmish with Spanish soldiers in the same year, but his prolific writing of unification and liberty remain a timeless vision and indelible influence today. Although he is considered one of Cuba's most venerable authors, it would be five years after his death before his writing was published outside of journals and newspapers.

Favianna Rodriguez

Elizabeth "Betita" Martínez

"The doctrine of Manifest Destiny facilitated the geographic extension and economic development of the United States while confirming racist policies and practices. It established White Supremacy more firmly than ever as central to the U.S. definition of itself. The arrogance of asserting that God gave white people (primarily men) the right to dominate everything around them still haunts our society and sustains its racist oppression."

ELIZABETH "BETITA" MARTÍNEZ IS a Chicana feminist activist, writer and community organizer. She has been working for social justice in the United States since the early days of the civil rights movement, when she worked as an organizer for the Student Non-Violent Coordinating Committee (SNCC), one of the most successful and influential organizations effecting change in the 1960s. Since her time with SNCC, Martínez has done much to identify white supremacy as a systemic issue in the United States, and to encourage collaboration amongst communities of color, focusing particularly on the voices of women and youth.

Martínez has worked as an editor for Simon & Schuster as well as *The Nation*, and has founded several publications that give voice to people of color. Her most influential work to date has been *500 Years of Chicano History in Pictures*. She continues to serve as a mentor for new generations of activists who are working to shape an anti-capitalist movement that is democratic and participatory, feminist, multi-racial, queer liberationist and internationalist.

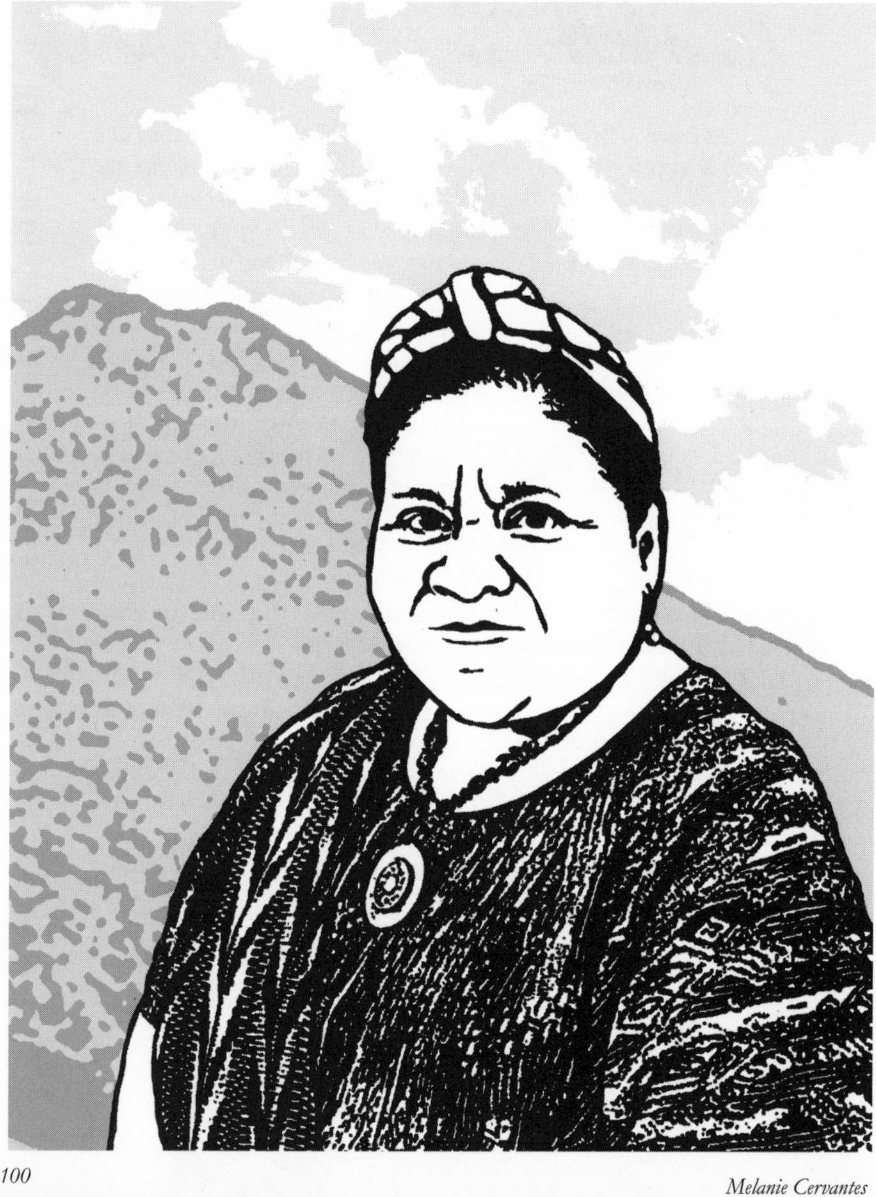

Melanie Cervantes

Rigoberta Menchú

"I'm still keeping my Indian identity a secret. I'm still keeping secret what I think no one should know. Not even anthropologists or intellectuals, no matter how many books they have, can find out all our secrets."

RIGOBERTA MENCHÚ TUM IS an Indigenous Quiche-Maya from Guatemala. As a youth, she helped her family with farm work and attended a Catholic school where she received an education up to the eighth grade. Outspoken on women's rights when she was only a teenager, Menchú has dedicated much of her life to campaigning against the brutality and human rights violations committed by the Guatemalan army from 1960-1996, during that country's civil war. In 1981, she escaped to Mexico after Guatemalan soldiers murdered most of her family.

In 1992, Menchú received the Nobel Peace Prize in recognition of her social justice and ethno-cultural reconciliation work, which is based on respect for the rights of Indigenous people worldwide. She participated in the preparation of the United Nations' "Declaration on the Rights of Indigenous Peoples" (adopted in 2007), and has been instrumental in bringing several key members of the Guatemalan military to international trial for genocide against the Mayan population. Menchú is involved in initiatives to bring low-cost generic medicine to rural areas and ran for the Guatemalan presidency in 2007. She continues to work as an advocate for Indigenous rights in Guatemala.

CHICO MENDES
MATARAM UM LIDER
MAS NÃO A LUTA

CHICO MENDES,
THEY KILLED OUR LEADER
BUT NOT OUR STRUGGLE!

Colin Matthes

Chico Mendes

"At first I thought I was fighting to save the rubber trees; then I thought I was fighting to save the Amazon rainforest. Now I realize I am fighting for humanity."

CHICO MENDES WAS A RUBBER tapper from Brazil whose organizing against the burning of the Amazon rainforest came to influence global environmental policy. Beginning in the 1960s, the price for rubber dropped and cattle ranchers began buying Amazonian land and burning off the vegetation to make room for cattle. Early on, Mendes would lead direct actions against clear-cutting. He would eventually found the first union of Brazilian rubber tappers called Xapuri Rural Workers' Union, bringing together native Brazilians who relied on rubber for their income. Mendes was a labor organizer with clear goals: to sustain communities of rubber tappers and Indigenous people and make accessible schools, jobs and healthcare. With a core focus on non-violence, Mendes put a tropical spin on the tactics of Gandhi and King, organizing the determined and peaceful resistance of rubber tappers to stand between the forest and forest-destroying cattle ranchers.

While forming partnerships with environmental groups, Mendes insisted on the importance of human rights, pioneering the combining of environmental and social justice movements. His death at the hands of a cattle-rancher's son brought international attention and worldwide support to the movement to save the Amazon rainforest. Brazil passed new environmental laws, and forest police began patrolling the Amazon to stop illegal cutting and burning. The 2.4 million-acre Chico Mendez Extractive Reserve was created, where 3,000 families now support themselves by gathering rubber and Brazil nuts.

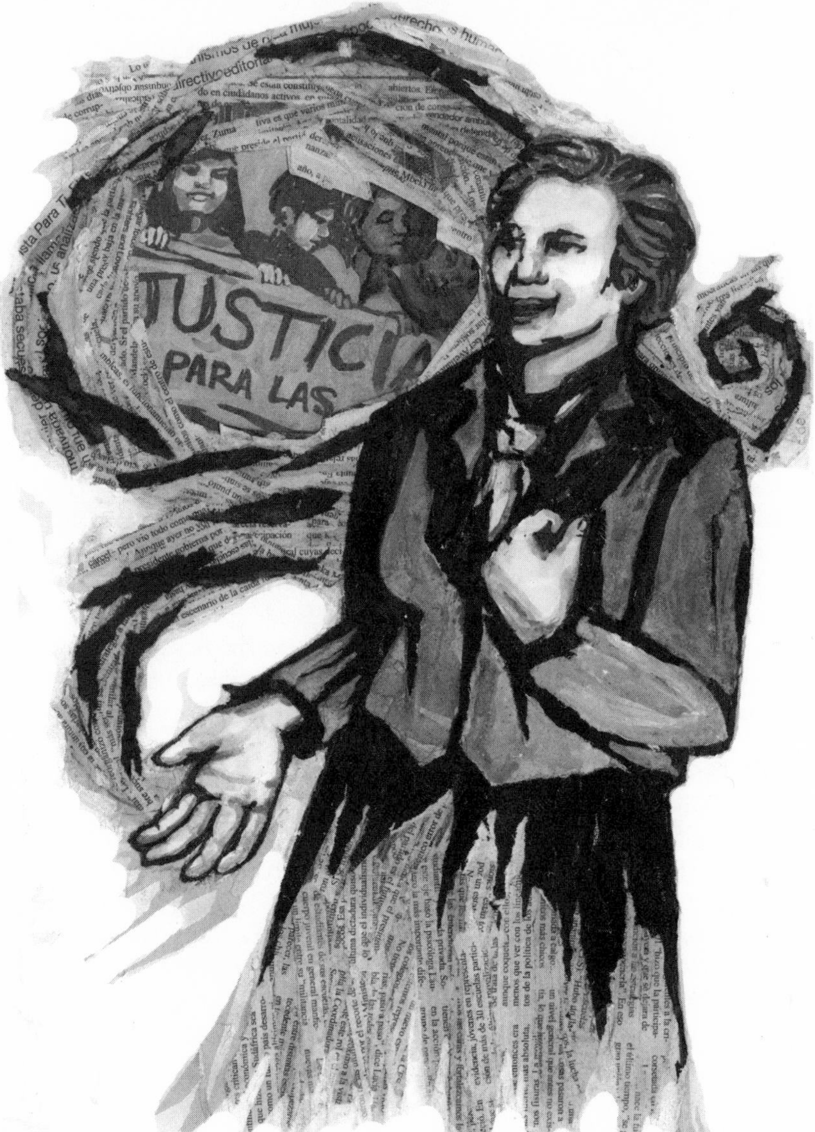
JUSTICIA
PARA LAS

Bec Young

Alicia Moreau de Justo

"We are moving towards that which has constituted the aspiration of the best of man: the suppression of privilege and violence, which engenders unnecessary pain, and the ardent desire for justice, peace and love, which man for centuries has placed in heaven, but which one day instead may become a reality in this world."

THE CHILD OF REFUGEES from the 1871 Paris Commune uprising, Alicia Moreau de Justo was born in London and immigrated to Argentina as a young woman. She studied medicine at the University of Buenos Aires and became one of the first doctors in Argentina to specialize in women's health. In her work with a variety of organizations and throughout her catalogue of published writings, Moreau advocated equality for all people. Along with her husband, Juan Bautista de Justo, she was a leading member of the Argentine Socialist party. She helped found the Socialist Confederation of Argentina and the National Feminist Union, among other organizations.

Moreau was among Argentina's most outspoken feminists and socialists of the past century. Traveling around Latin America, she used her knowledge and social position as a medical doctor to organize against the exploitation of women in the sex trade and to encourage public sex education, government-sponsored day care centers and maternity protection. She also spoke passionately for the equal treatment of women in the workplace, in politics and in the home. In her nineties, she was an active member of the *Asamblea Permanente por los Derechos Humanos* (Permanent Assembly for Human Rights), with whom she protested the disappearance of thousands of Argentines during the military dictatorship of 1976-1983, also known as The Dirty War.

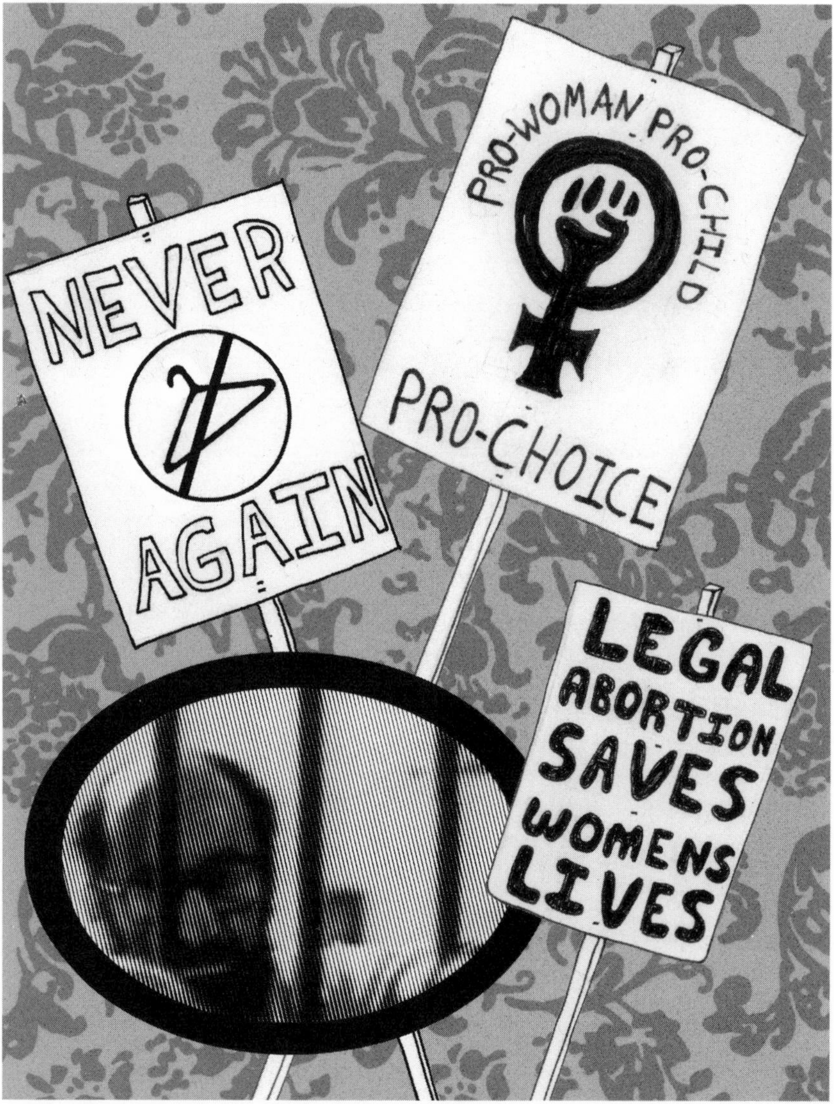
NEVER AGAIN
PRO-WOMAN PRO-CHILD
PRO-CHOICE
LEGAL ABORTION SAVES WOMENS LIVES

Jesse Purcell

Henry Morgentaler

{March 19, 1923 - Present}

"Every mother a willing mother. Every child a wanted child."

HENRY MORGENTALER, BORN IN Poland, spent his early life under Nazi rule in a Jewish ghetto. Eventually imprisoned and shuffled through several concentration camps, he survived his father and mother and was liberated, along with his brother, by the U.S. army in 1945. While the UN attempted to have Germany pay reparations by offering scholarships to survivors of the concentration camps, Morgentaler found a strong anti-Semitism persisted.

In 1950, Morgentaler and his wife, Chava, immigrated to Canada where he graduated from Université de Montréal as a medical doctor. For nearly 20 years he practiced family medicine in a working class neighborhood in the east end of Montréal. In 1967, Morgentaler publicly spoke in favor of changing the abortion law before a government committee. After his announcement, his best friend's daughter approached him, requesting he perform for her what would be his first illegal abortion. He started performing abortions in his clinic, and in 1973 appeared on television again to announce that he had performed over 5,000 illegal abortions. This prompted numerous legal battles, including the temporary legalization of abortion when deemed medically necessary, and the eventual decriminalization of abortion in 1988.

Morgentaler firmly places his views of abortion within a wider social justice analysis. His father, a member of the internationalist Jewish Socialist Bund, had a great influence on his beliefs. In addition to his activism around abortion, Morgentaler is an outspoken critic of the state of Israel and was the first president of the Humanist Association of Canada. Over his lifetime, Morgentaler has encountered numerous death threats, attacks, and bombings, though he continues to fight for accessible and safe abortions in Canada.

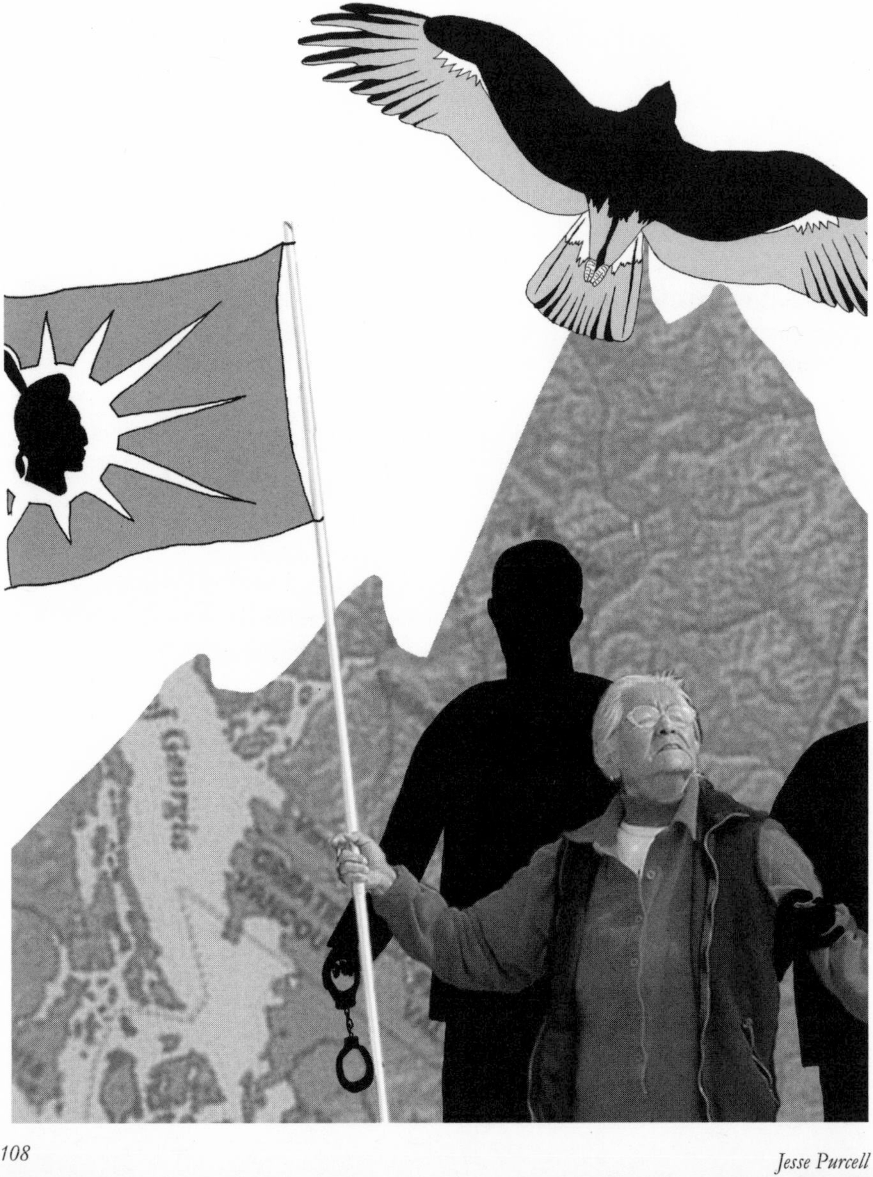

Jesse Purcell

Harriet Nahanee

"What I would like to see is people with [traditional] knowledge to teach the small, little people how to grow up with pride. This generation is lost. My generation is lost—they're assimilated. They don't think like an Indian. What I'd like to see is our five-year-olds being taught their language, their songs, their games, their spirituality, their Indian, eh, their Indian-ness. I'd like to ask all the people out there to reclaim their culture—practice it, teach the children, and let's reclaim our backbone, our culture and put some pride in our children."

HARRIET NAHANEE, AN ELDER of the Pacheedaht and Squamish Nations, believed she had an inherited and sacred duty to protect the land, water and air for future generations. Like many First Nations people, she was taken as a child and interned in church-run boarding schools funded by the Canadian government. There, Native children were routinely punished for singing traditional songs and speaking their languages. Many also endured malnourishment, physical and sexual assault. She later spoke out against these schools as part of a broader system of assimilating Indigenous people, fracturing families, destabilizing communities and creating a legacy of dependency.

Nahanee became central figure in opposing highway extensions into Eagleridge Bluffs, a tract of wetland habitat in Squamish territory (a result of B.C. hosting the 2010 Olympics on unceded Native land). In 2006 she defied an injunction and visited the land to sing death songs and say prayers for the dying habitat. The following year, she and several other activists were arrested for blockading construction traffic on the highway. Nahanee refused to recognize the authority of the court. Jailed in substandard facilities that aggravated her already weakened immune system, she fell ill with pneumonia a week after her release and died shortly after. Nahanee's actions and courage inspired many Indigenous people in the area to organize, mobilize and educate one another for the future.

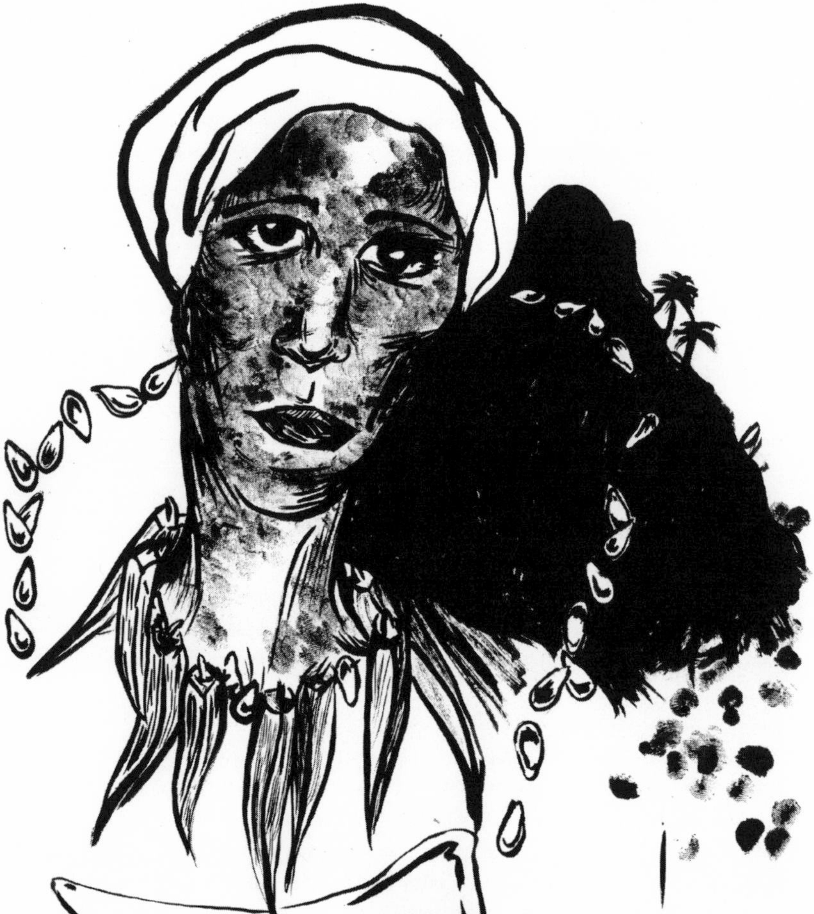

Nanny of the Maroons

"And when my training was over, Nanny tells us, they circled my waist with pumpkin seeds / and dried okra, a traveler's jigida, / and sold me to the traders / all my weapons within me. / I was sent, tell that to history." - Lorna Goodison

VERY LITTLE IS KNOWN of Nanny's early life, except that she was born in Africa's Gold Coast, likely of the Ashanti tribes, and came to Jamaica as a slave. Her story is an example of history passed down almost entirely through oral tradition, with most written accounts coming from colonial British sources. The power of this oral tradition speaks to the importance of storytelling as a potent component of communities of resistance, contributing to their strength and spiritual health.

The Maroons were escaped African slaves who formed autonomous communities in colonized regions of the "New World." Jamaican Maroon leaders drew directly upon the African traditions of courage and determination, which ran counter to the prevailing stigma of inferiority wrought by the new colonial military powers. In Jamaica, two distinct communities of Maroons arose in spite of British colonial rule: the Windward Maroons, led by Nanny, and the Leeward Maroons, led by Nanny's brother, Cudjoe. Nanny's settlement was ensconced in a mountaintop area that became known as Nanny Town, remarkable for being strategically positioned against the approach of colonial troops. Nanny and the fugitives in her command conducted raids against British plantations to procure supplies and to free a continual stream of enslaved Africans. Committed to liberation, Nanny herself is credited with freeing as many as 800 slaves in her lifetime. In one popular story, during a time of starvation while the Maroons were on the brink of surrender to the British, Nanny had visionary dream. She awoke to find pumpkin seeds in her pocket. She planted them along a hillside, and within weeks they provided crucial sustenance for the Maroons.

AND YOU WILL ASK;
WHY DOESN'T HIS POETRY
OR & SPEAK OF DREAMS & LEAVES
THE GREAT VOLCAN
HIS NATIVE LAND?
COME & SEE THE BLOOD
IN THE STREETS
COME AND SEE
THE BLOOD IN
THE STREETS
COME AND
SEE
THE BLOOD
IN
THE
STREETS!

Erik Ruin

Pablo Neruda

"I have always wanted the hands of the people to be seen in poetry. I have always preferred a poetry where the fingerprints show. A poetry of loam, where water can sing. A poetry of bread, where everyone may eat."

PABLO NERUDA, BORN RICARDO Elicier Neftali Reyes Basoalto, was one of Latin America's most beloved poets. He made a name for himself at age 20 with the publication of the erotic *Viente Poemas de Amor y Una Cancion Desesperada* (*Twenty Love Poems and A Desperate Song*) in 1924, still his best-selling work. Later books, most famously *Residencia en La Tierra* (1947) and *Canto General* (1950) would explore themes of nature, death, Indigenous culture and class struggle in vivid, sentimental and at times hallucinatory language. He was awarded the Nobel Prize for Literature in 1971, which was somewhat controversial given his political views.

Serving at the Chilean consulate in Madrid when the Spanish Civil War broke out, Neruda was politicized by the struggle against fascism. He organized alliances of anti-fascist intellectuals, wrote the fiery *Spain In My Heart*, worked for Republican newspapers and later helped organize the immigration of Republican refugees to Chile. Neruda had a long political career as a diplomat. He was elected to the Chilean Congress as a Communist Party candidate in 1945, though was forced into exile when President Gonzalez Videla outlawed the Communist Party in 1948. Later, he served as Chile's ambassador to France under Salvador Allende from 1970-73. Neruda died of prostate cancer in 1973, shortly after the military coup that deposed Allende and instituted the Pinochet dictatorship. His funeral served as a site of protest against the new regime, whose military forces had harassed the dying poet. Thousands of Chileans defied an imposed curfew to accompany the poet to his grave while openly weeping, reciting his verses and joyously singing the *Internationale*.

{JULY 12, 1904 - SEPTEMBER 23, 1973}

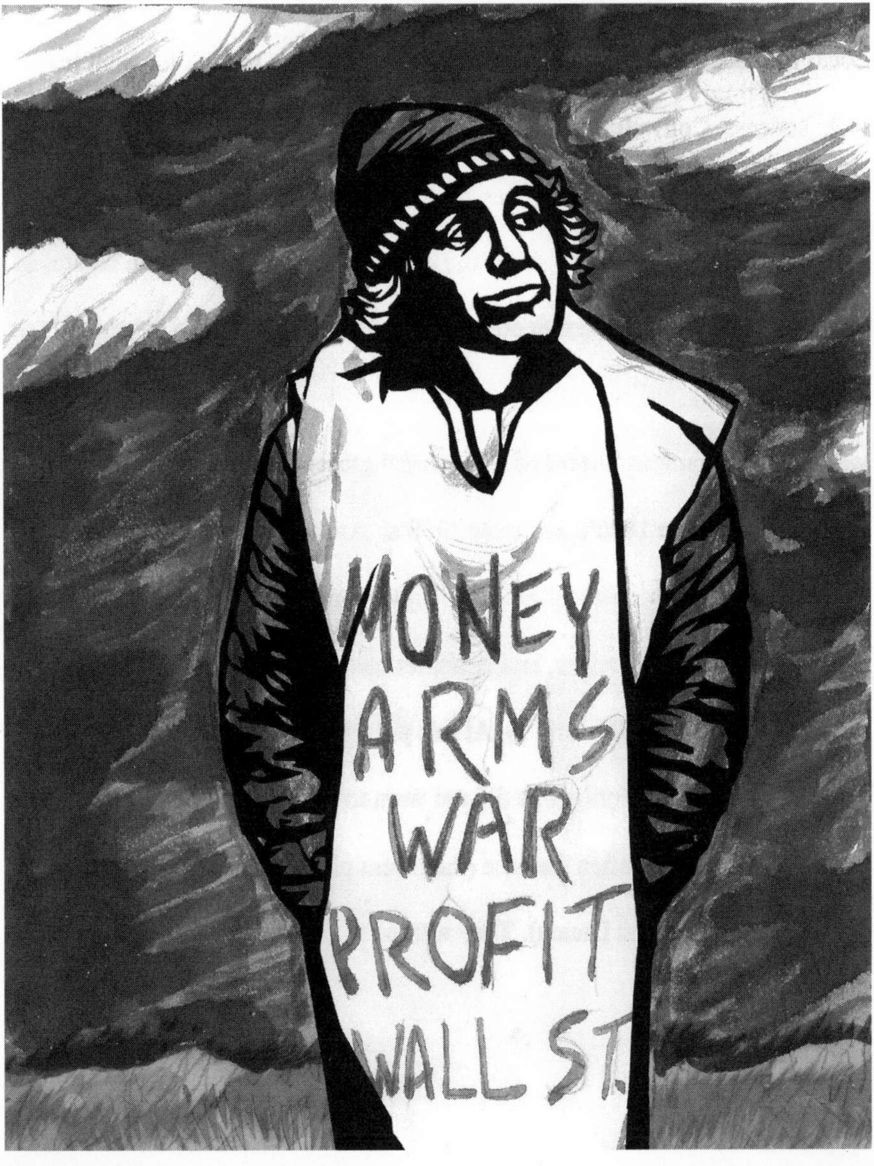
MONEY
ARMS
WAR
PROFIT
WALL ST.

Erik Ruin

"I was a woman writing at the early moment when small drops of worried resentment and noble rage were secretly, slowly building into the second wave of the women's movement. I didn't know my small drop presence or usefulness in this accumulation…The great wave would crest half a generation later, leaving men sputtering and anxious, but somewhat improved for the crashing bath. Every woman writing in these years has had to swim in that feminist wave, no matter what she thinks of it, even if she swims bravely against it, she has been supported by it—the buoyancy, the noise, the saltiness."

GRACE PALEY WAS A POET, short story writer and activist raised in the Bronx by Ukrainian Jewish parents. Though best known for her collections of short stories, she was initially drawn to poetry and studied briefly with the influential English poet W.H. Auden. Paley didn't begin to write prose until the age of 30, and was 37 when her first collection, *The Little Disturbances of Man*, was published.

Her stories are rooted in the everyday lives of women and were written in vernacular, and an often subtly humorous tone. They shine with a deep love of humanity and carry compassionate critiques of restrictive gender roles, self-righteous activism, race and class divides and the military-industrial complex. With a sense of humor about even her own values, Paley also used her writing to make fun of self-righteous activism. Paley was active in feminist, anti-war, anti-nuclear and environmental movements up until her death, and participated in the War Resister's League, the Women's Pentagon Actions, the Clamshell Alliance and Bread & Puppet Theater.

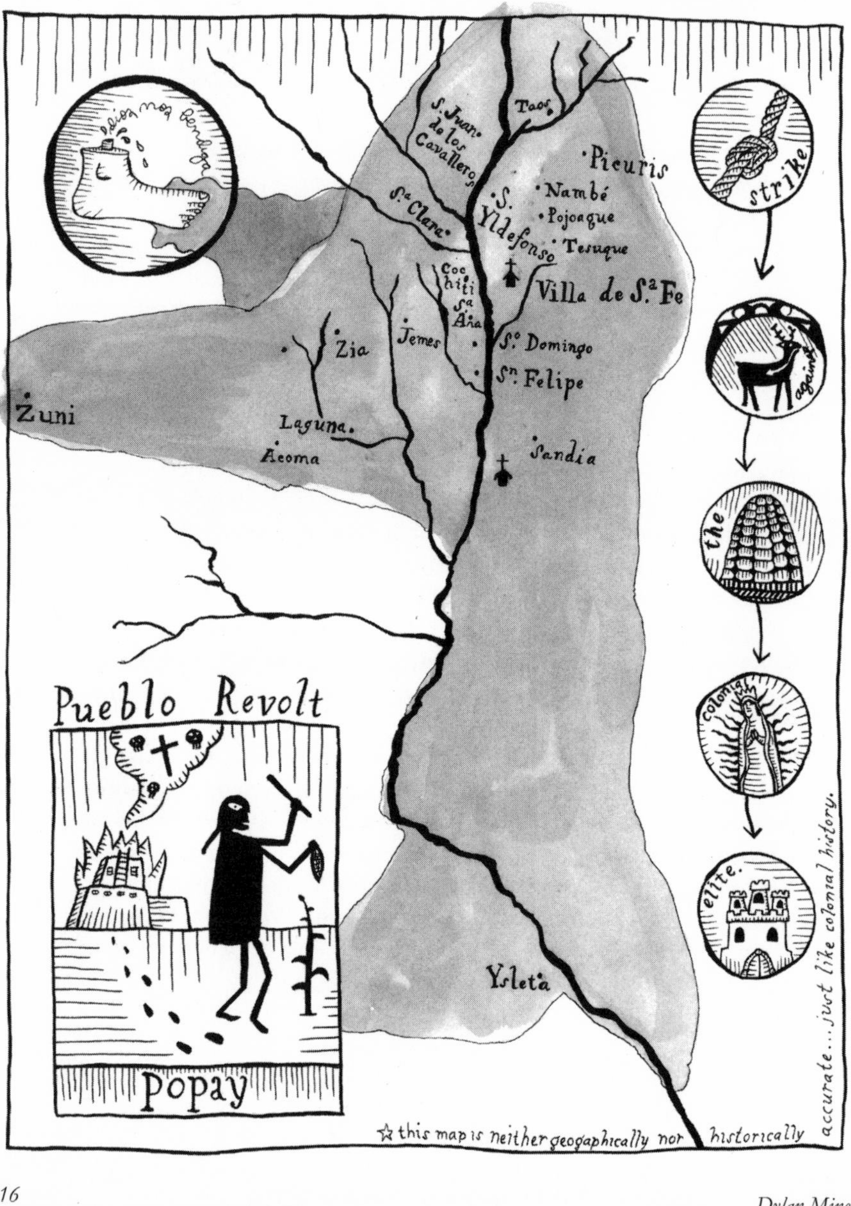
dios nos bendiga
Taos
S. Juan de los Cavalleros
Picuris
Nambé
Pojoaque
S. Yldefonso
Sa Clara
Tesuque
Cochiti
Villa de Sa. Fe
Sa Aña
Zia
Jemes
So Domingo
Sn. Felipe
Zuni
Laguna
Acoma
Sandia
Ysleta
Pueblo Revolt
Popay
strike
against
the
colonial
elite.
☆ this map is neither geogaphically nor historically accurate... just like colonial history.

"One leader perhaps said to another that the man from Oke Owinge has 'the cunning of the fox and the heart of the bear'...according to tradition, it was said that Po'pay was not arrogant but instead was always willing to learn, consider advice and to explain his decisions." -Joe Sando, *Pueblo Profiles*

PO'PAY WAS A TEWA spiritual leader who led the 1680 Pueblo Revolt, an anti-colonial movement to remove the Spanish political and cultural presence in the area we now know as New Mexico. Born Popyn, meaning "ripe squash" in the Tewa-language spoken in Ohkay Owingeh (San Juan Pueblo), Po'pay was an important activist and community leader. Following the arrival of Spanish settlers in mid-16th century, a colonial capital was established in 1598 at Ohkay Owingeh. After nearly a century of oppressive interactions, Spanish colonizers convicted 50 Indigenous leaders of practicing "sorcery," the word they used to describe all non-Catholic religious beliefs. Following the public and violent punishment of the "sorcerers," it was the direct action of local communities that forced the Spanish authorities to release the prisoners, though two had already been killed and a third had taken his own life.

Upon his release from jail, Po'pay moved north to Taos, where in 1680 he organized a successful assault on the colonial administration. Beginning in Santa Fe, thousands of Indigenous warriors engaged in a 10-day offensive that forced the Hispanic community (including Tlaxcala servants, *mestizo* residents, *genízaros* (detribalized natives) and Pueblo allies) to relocate hundreds of miles south to El Paso del Norte. Their retreat however, would be short lived, but the anti-colonial struggles of Po'pay and his contemporaries forever changed the relationship between native and settler societies in New Mexico. In 2005, Tewa artist Cliff Fragua of Jemez Pueblo completed a statue of Po'pay that resides in the National Statuary Hall in Washington, D.C..

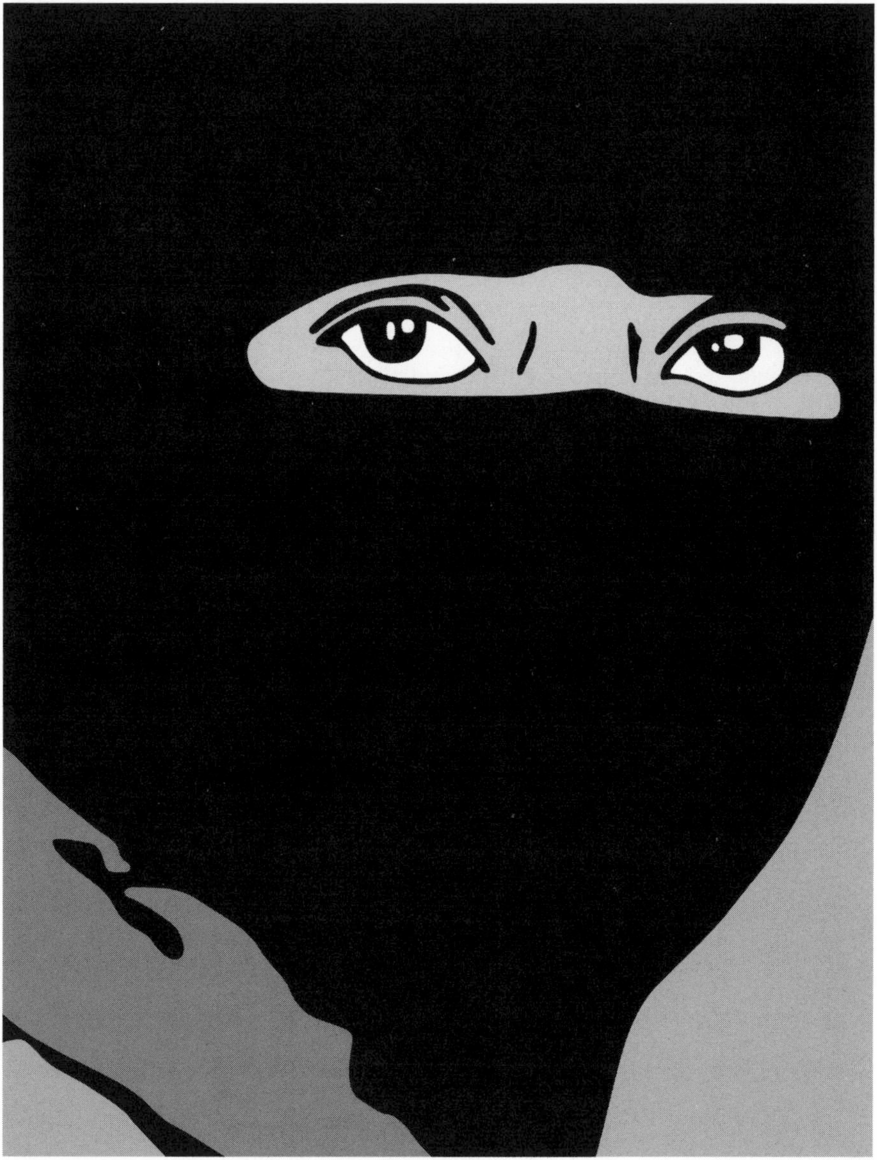

Jesus Barraza

Comandante Ramona

{1959 - JANUARY 6, 2006}

"¡Todo Somos Ramona!"

COMANDANTE RAMONA WAS A Tzotzil Indian born in Chiapas, Mexico. There is very little known about her life prior to joining the EZLN, or *Ejercito Zapatista de Liberacion Nacional* (Zapatista Army for National Liberation), in which she was a Commander. On January 1, 1994, the EZLN went public, announcing control of several towns in the Mexican state of Chiapas, the same day the North American Free Trade Agreement (NAFTA) went into effect. In February 1994, after 13 days of war between the EZLN and Mexico, Comandante Ramona was sent to the first peace talks. She quickly gained popularity as a woman warrior from the South. In the years following the 1994 uprising, she dealt with serious kidney problems, traveling between Chiapas and Mexico City for hospital visits. Her illness remained a serious issue throughout her life although she continued to organize until her death.

It was during Comandante Ramona's trip to Mexico City, to participate in a meeting of the National Indigenous Conference in 1996, that the support of the people was demonstrated. Although the EZLN was banned from participating in the meeting, Ramona was sent to represent the Zapatistas. To ensure that she was not arrested, supporters formed a security ring around her. During that trip Ramona addressed a crowd of over 100,000 supporters, with people chanting, "We are all Ramona," demonstrating the mythical role that she had taken in society.

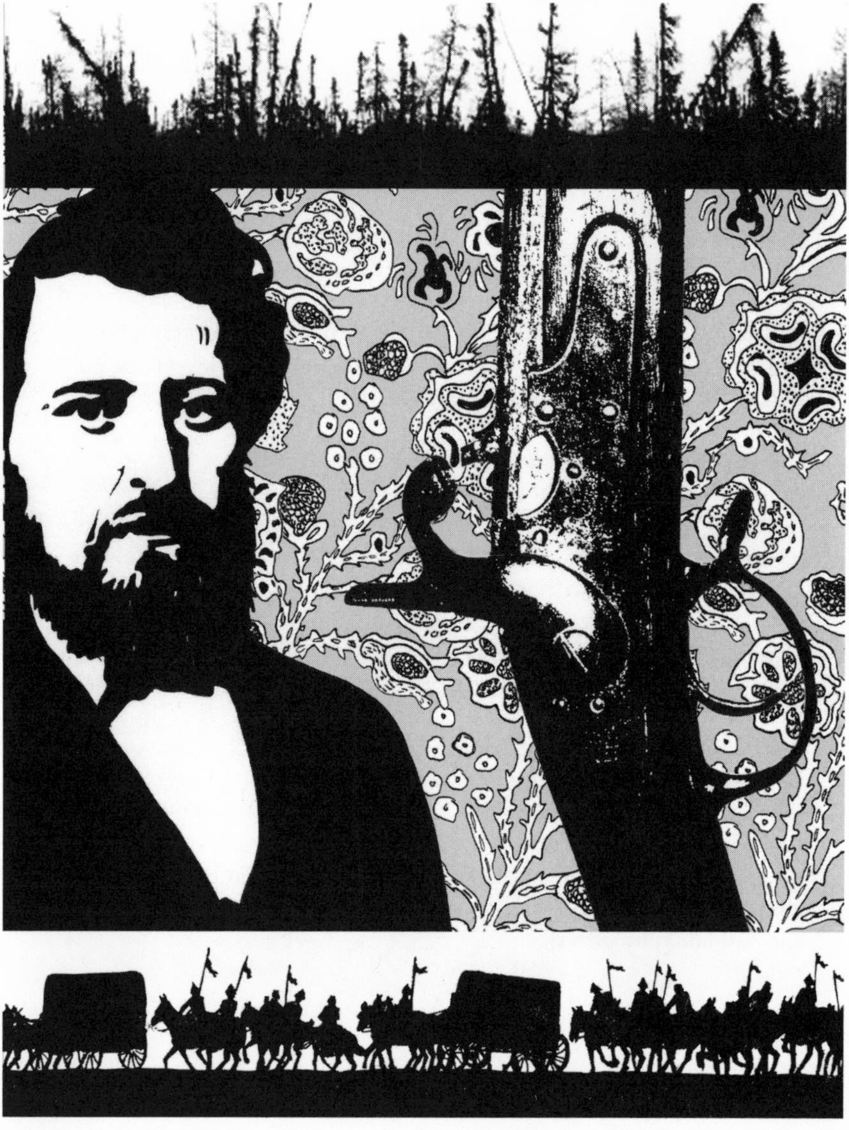

Jesse Purcell

Louis Riel

{OCTOBER 22, 1844 – NOVEMBER 16, 1885}

"My people will sleep for 100 years, and when they awake, it will be the artists who give them back their spirit."

LOUIS RIEL WAS A Métis leader, strategist and, later in life, self-proclaimed prophet who fought actively against the western expansion of Anglophone settlers in what would become Canada. At age 25, Riel was instrumental in the Red River Resistance, a militant Métis action to preserve land in opposition to the sprawling control of the Canadian Confederation. The actions at Red River saw the birth of the province of Manitoba, for a time securing land for Métis until speculators began once again to encroach westward.

In his later years, Riel came to see himself as a divinely ordained leader of the Métis. In 1884, after being elected to Parliament but remaining in exile for fear of assassination, Riel was found living and raising a family in Montana. In the U.S., he involved himself in local Montana politics and particularly concerned himself with working against the alcohol trade, which he saw as contributing to the decimation of his people. Asked to negotiate for Saskatchewan Métis and other natives as he had done at Red River, Riel saw an opportunity to create a Métis homeland, but the Canadian government sent soldiers instead of negotiators. Several months of guerilla warfare against the Canadian military followed, however many of Riel's allies fled or surrendered and the effort did not succeed. Riel was found guilty of treason but refused to plead insanity and was executed in 1885.

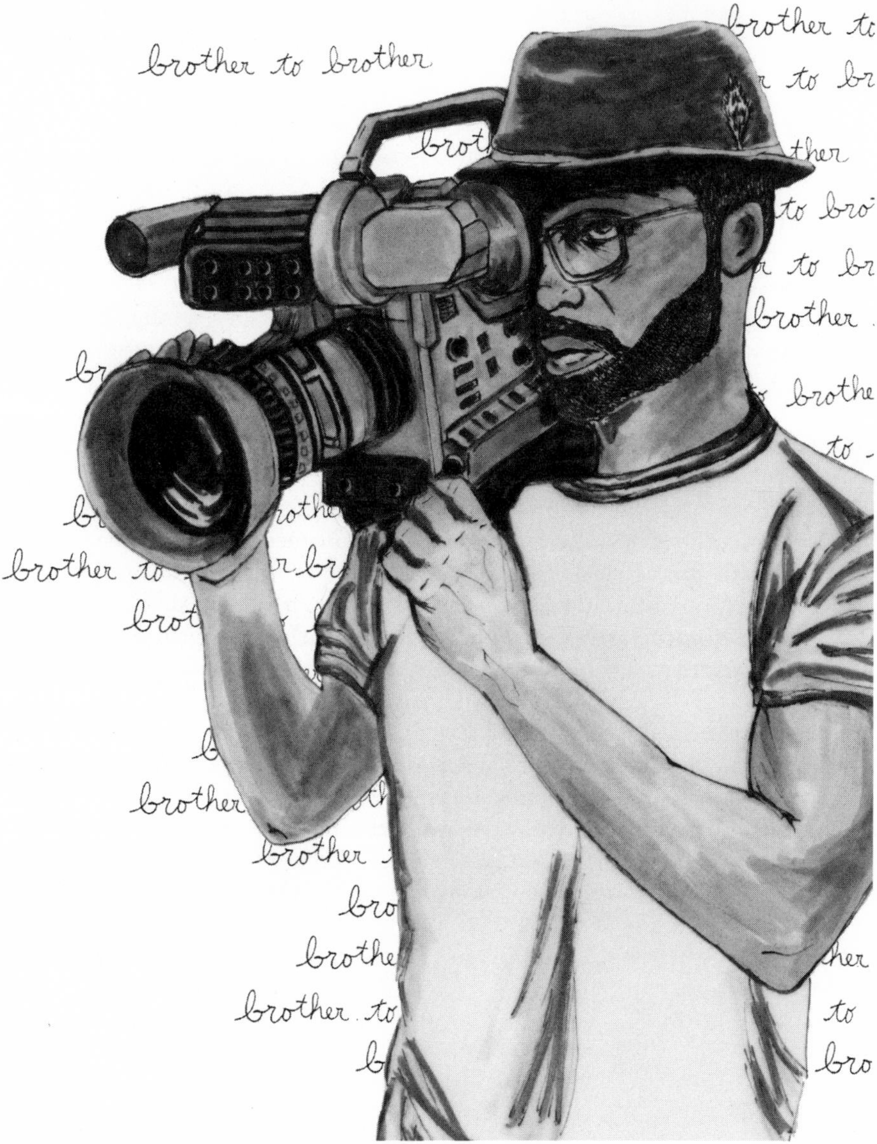
brother to brother

Molly Fair

Marlon Riggs

{February 3, 1957 - April 5, 1994}

"Whenever we speak the truths of our lives, our words must be more than mere words: Every time we speak, we must engage in the most radical—as in fundamental—form of self-affirmation. As communities historically oppressed through silence, through the power of Voice we must seize our freedom, achieve our fullest humanity."

MARLON RIGGS WAS BORN to a military family in Fort Worth, Texas and spent most of his childhood outside of the United States. He returned to attend college at Harvard University, where he began increasing his visibility and self-expression as an African-American gay man. As a poet, he was drawn to filmmaking as a medium he could use as a platform to express his views on racism and homophobia. Central to Riggs' work was a critical analysis of the portrayals of African-American homosexuality in popular media and the struggles of gay men within the black community in the U.S..

Riggs' documentary *Ethnic Notions* is a particularly incendiary look at racist imagery in American history and contemporary popular culture, and his later award-winning documentary *Color Adjustment* specifically targets problematic and detrimental stereotypes in prime-time television. His experimental film *Tongues Untied*, which confronted homophobia within African-American communities and explored black gay male identity, was critically acclaimed yet assailed by conservative groups and policy-makers. Banned from numerous public-broadcasting stations, Riggs' work sparked debates about funding and censorship in public television, and encouraged him to rally support for a more inclusive, diverse popular media. After contracting the HIV virus, Riggs became an outspoken AIDS activist, exploring his experiences in his film *Non, Je Ne Regrette Rien* (*No, I Regret Nothing*). He continued to work on his film *Black Is... Black Ain't*, a personal journey and examination of a myriad of African-American identities, until his death in 1994.

I'M NOT MISSING
A MINUTE OF THIS,
IT'S THE
REVOLUTION!
—Sylvia Rivera

Sylvia Rivera

SYLVIA RIVERA, BORN REY Rivera Mendoza, was a transgender civil rights activist from the Bronx, New York. She left her troubled home life as a child and found a new family within the community of drag queens on the street. She came into political activism in the 1960s, fighting against police repression and brutality towards the gay community. Rivera was at the forefront of the pivotal Stonewall Riots in 1969, became involved in the nascent gay liberation movement. She then became vocal about the exclusion of transgender rights within the agenda of the Gay Activists Alliance. She also formed important connections with other radicals in the Young Lords and Black Panther Party.

As a Latina, her experiences made her more focused on issues of poverty and discrimination faced by people of color, and led to her advocate for people marginalized within society at large and LGBT communities. Together with her friend Marsha P. Johnson, Rivera founded the Street Transvestite Action Revolutionaries (STAR) in 1970, a radical group dedicated to providing support and shelter to homeless transgender youth.

Rivera left NYC and activism for a time, battling substance abuse. Upon return, she lived with the homeless queer community on the Christopher Street piers. She later moved to the Transy House Collective in Brooklyn, a home modeled on the STAR house, and resumed her political activism. In 2000 at the Millennium March, she was acclaimed as the Mother of all gay people. She re-established STAR in the early 2000s, using direct action tactics to fight for the rights of the trans community, people of color, issues of homelessness, and AIDS. Even on her deathbed, she continued to pressure the Human Rights Campaign to include transgender identity in New York State's sexual orientation non-discrimination legislation.

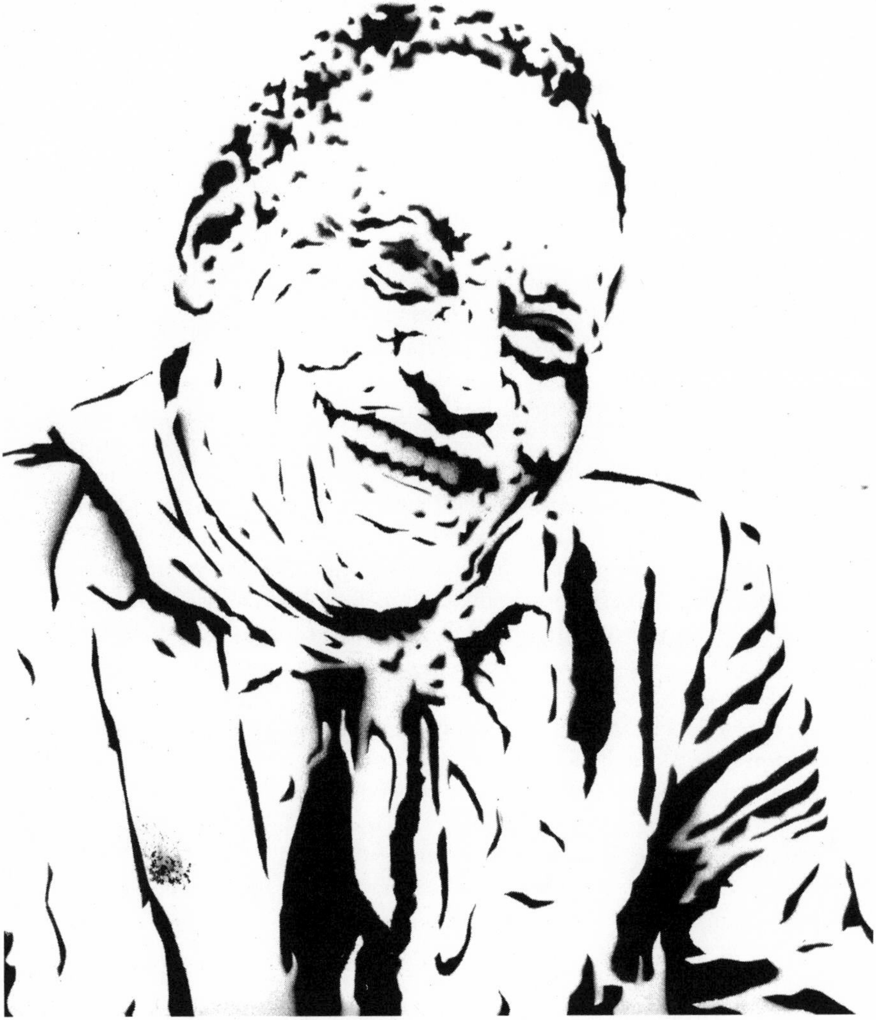

Chris Stain

"As an artist I come to sing, but as a citizen, I will always speak for peace, and no one can silence me in this."

PAUL ROBESON WAS A GIFTED actor, athlete, writer, singer and stage performer. He gained celebrity status before the United States had seen the struggles of the civil rights movement, and the country was in many ways unprepared for an accomplished African-American to speak out so consistently against racism, war and injustice. In the 1940s, with minstrel shows still prevalent in American entertainment, Robeson saw success on stage as the first black Othello in the long-running Broadway production of the Shakespeare play, and went on to portray African-Americans in dignified film roles that Hollywood had never previously intended. He spoke and performed songs in churches, union halls, synagogues and schools, and toured the world learning about working class and Indigenous struggles and bringing those stories back to the U.S..

Later, as Robeson became world-renowned as an activist, his open intentions to utilize his fame to speak out against capitalism and oppression kept him under continual surveillance by U.S. and British agencies for the majority of his adult life. He was blacklisted for his support of international socialist and communist struggles, his passport was revoked from 1950-58 and his athletic and entertainment record have nearly been wiped from mainstream availability or recognition. However, Robeson's legacy of personal and professional integrity still shines on as a positive example for aspiring artists and athletes.

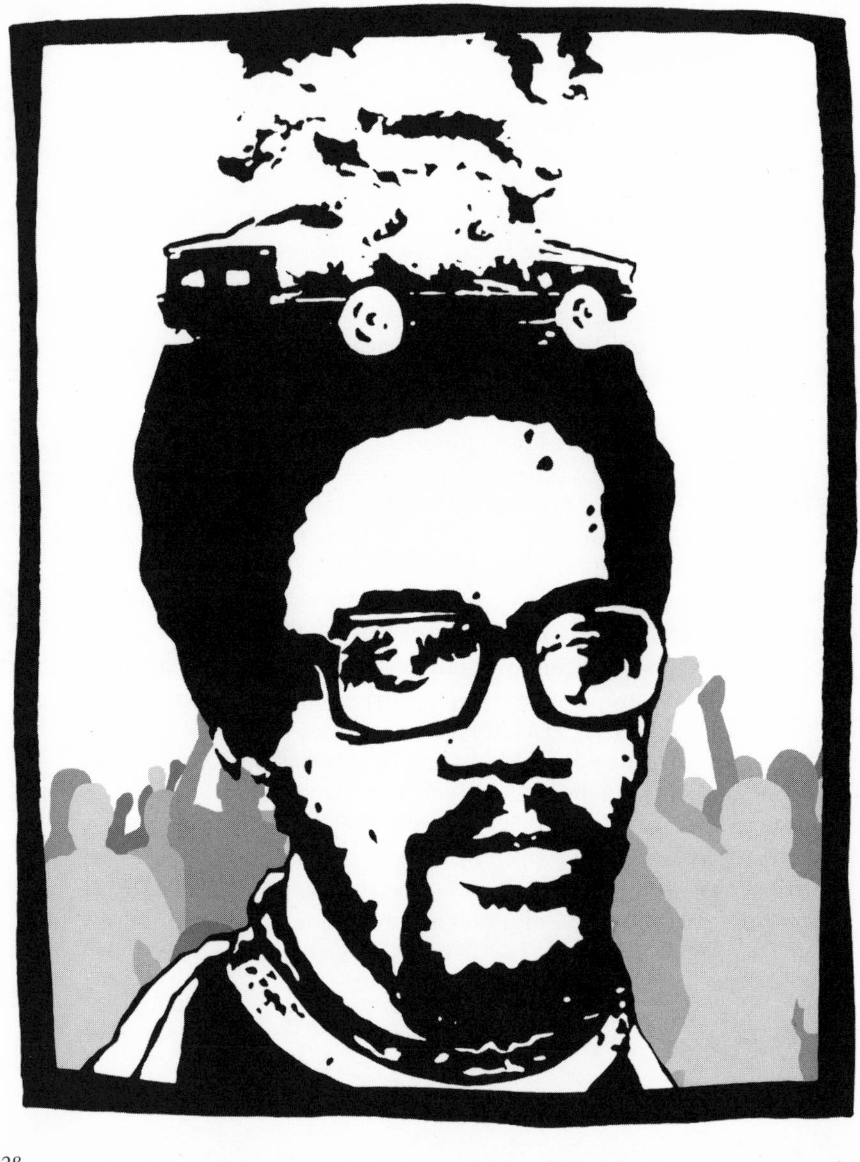

Josh MacPhee

Walter Rodney

"What I am trying to say is this: The revolution is made by ordinary people, not by angels, made by people from all walks of life, and more particularly by the working class who are in the majority. And it is a sign of the times, the sign of the power of revolutionary transformation, when a street force [i.e. gang] member is developed into a fighting cadre in a political movement."

WALTER RODNEY WAS A Guyanese author, teacher and revolutionary. He is most well-known for his book *How Europe Underdeveloped Africa*, a foundational text in defining and explaining neo-colonialism and the economic limitations on African independence from the West. In the 1960s and 70s, Rodney taught at the University of Dar-es-Salaam in Tanzania, and in the early 70s returned to the Caribbean. He was banned from teaching in his native Guyana, so he took a post at the University of the West Indies in Jamaica.

His teachings and writings on the importance of black Americans understanding the history of Africa and his particular Pan-Africanist brand of Black Power were extremely popular with the poor, working class and an increasingly revolutionary sector of Rastafarian groups. Before he had even been there a year, the Jamaican government banned him from the country, leading to what are now known as the 1968 "Rodney Riots" in Kingston. Rodney finally returned to Guyana, where he was supposed to take up a teaching position prior to the government canceling his appointment. Instead he became deeply involved in political organizing and helped found the Working People's Alliance. In 1979, he was arrested and charged with arson of government buildings. Before the trial, Rodney was killed by a bomb planted in his car.

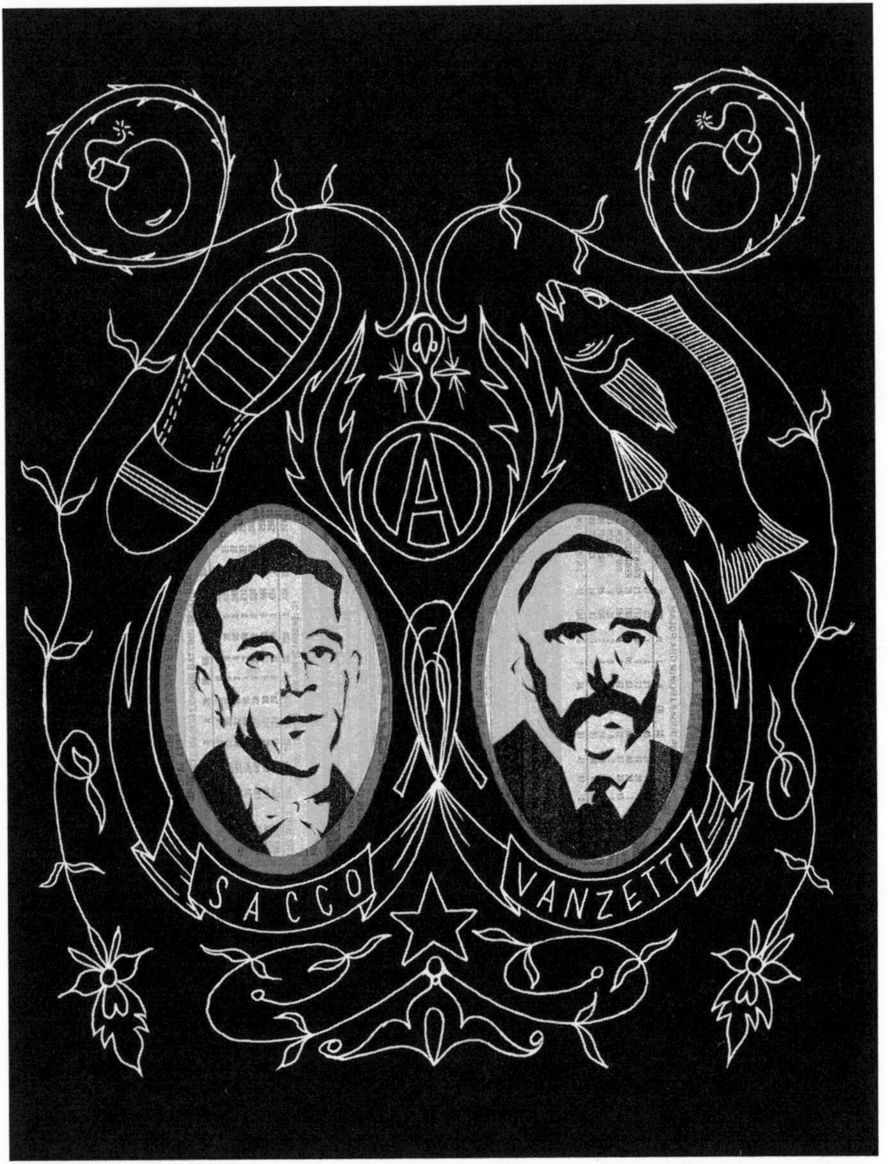
SACCO
VANZETTI

Sacco & Vanzetti

"If it had not been for this, I might have lived out my life, talking at street corners to scorning men. I might have died, unmarked, unknown, a failure. Now we are not a failure. This is our career and our triumph. Never in our full life can we do such a work for tolerance, for justice, for man's understanding of man, as we now do by accident. Our words—our lives—our pains—nothing! The taking of our lives—lives of a good shoemaker and a poor fishpeddler—all! The last moment belongs to us—that agony is our triumph!" - Bartolomeo Vanzetti

FERDINANDO NICOLA SACCO AND Bartolomeo Vanzetti were Italian-born anarchists who arrived in the U.S. in 1908. By trade, Sacco was a cobbler and Vanzetti a fish seller. Both were followers of Luigi Galleani, an Italian anarchist, publisher of the newspaper *Cronaca Sovversiva* and public agitator who called for bombings and assassinations in support of revolution. In 1919, Galleani was deported and most of his supporters went underground. It is in this context that on April 15, 1920 a payroll hold-up occurred in Braintree, Massachusetts during which the paymaster and security guard were both killed. Sacco and Vanzetti were arrested for the action. Multiple trials and appeals later, they were found guilty and executed by electric chair on August 23, 1927.

Today there is significant evidence that they did not commit the crime, and few contest that their trial was grossly unjust. During the trial they did not shy away from their anarchist beliefs or their commitment to revolutionary violence. A massive international protest movement developed in support of Sacco and Vanzetti. During the entire ordeal and after their deaths there were a number of attacks on banks and sites of capitalism, including the 1920 bombing of Wall Street, which was carried out by other Galleanists and killed thirty people. Significantly less violent support occurred as well, particularly a large outpouring of pro-Sacco and Vanzetti cultural activity including plays, movies, novels, music, poetry, paintings and murals telling their story.

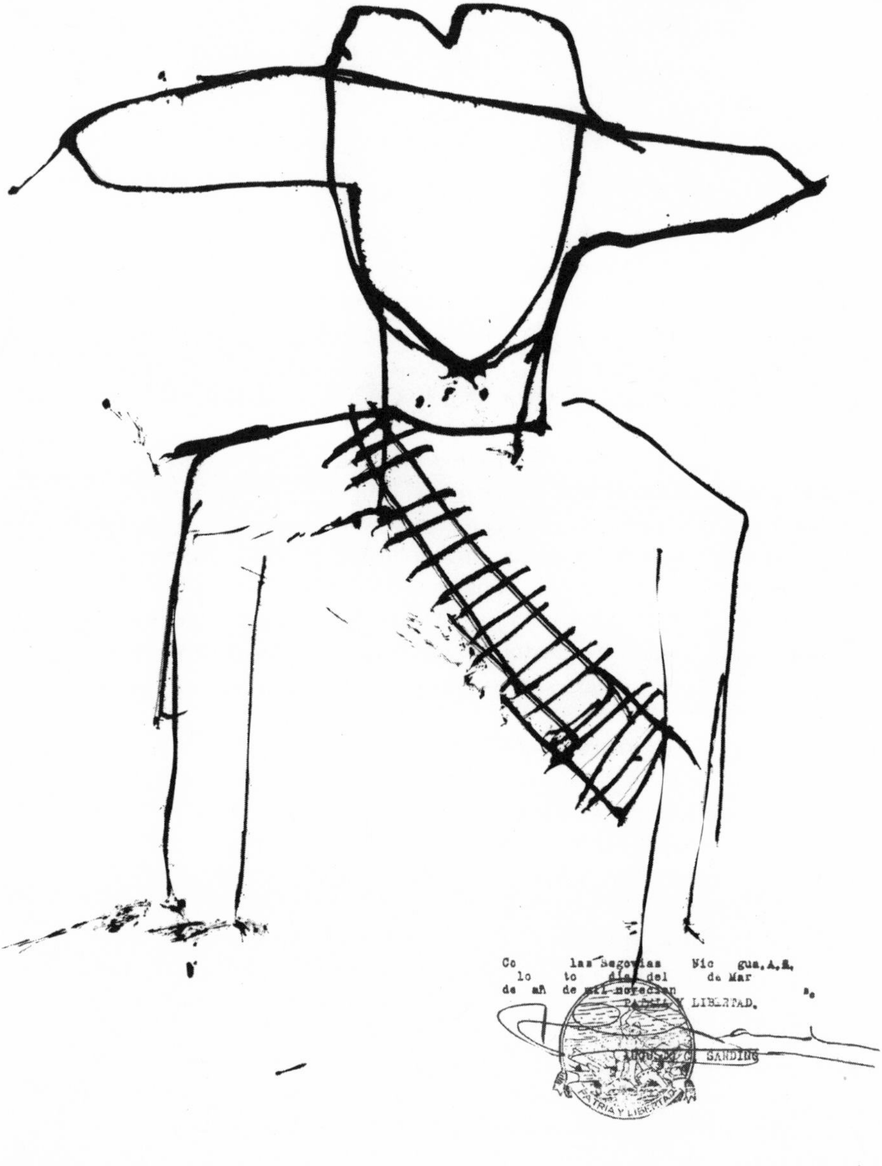
Co las Segovias Nic gua, A.S.
lo to del de Mar
de añ de
LIBERTAD.
PATRIA Y LIBERTAD

Augusto César Sandino

"Only dead can one be a hero always, and a symbol beside. That is to say, dead, one can also contribute, perhaps even more."

AUGUSTO CÉSAR SANDINO WAS a Nicaraguan guerilla who led a militant indigenous struggle against U.S. Marines until 1933, when the United States withdrew from his homeland. Born out of wedlock to a plantation owner and his servant, Sandino was eventually abandoned by both parents. While in Mexico in his mid-twenties, he witnessed the Mexican Revolution. Charged by the communist and anarchist elements there, he began to see the shape of a struggle that he felt should embrace all of Latin America. He returned to Nicaragua to work in a gold mine, eventually organizing the workers there in a revolt against the mine owner and going on to lead a volunteer army against U.S. occupational forces.

Sandino's knowledge of the Nicaraguan terrain and skillful military leadership made it difficult for U.S. Marines to counter his army's homespun guerilla tactics. His millenarian spirituality was a key influence on his revolutionary ideology, and he saw the trials of his army in Nicaragua as part of a universal struggle towards divine justice and unified racial harmony. His image and life have become symbolic of struggles against imperialism, his trademark hat in particular a common icon in protest graffiti in South America.

In 1934, after peace negotiations with the newly democratically-elected Nicaraguan President Sacasa, which would see Sandino's forces lay down their arms and obtain amnesty and communal farmland, he was assassinated on orders from then National Guard director Anastasio Somoza Garcia. The Somoza family regime ruled for 40 years, until 1979, when the *Frente Sandinista de Liberación Nacional* (Sandinista National Liberation Front) overthrew Somoza's son and installed a socialist government in his place.

"It is our duty to fight for our freedom. It is our duty to win. We must love each other and support each other. We have nothing to lose but our chains."

Melanie Cervantes

Assata Shakur

{July 16, 1947 - Present}

ASSATA SHAKUR, BORN JOANNE Byron, never finished high school, but obtained a GED and went on to receive a college degree at the same time as her radical activism blossomed. She joined the Black Panther Party and later the Black Liberation Army (BLA), and maintained a consistent critique of the gender dynamics within both organizations throughout her involvement. In her mid-twenties, she became the subject of a nationwide FBI hunt that sought to link her to any and all violent crimes involving a black woman on the East Coast, part of the covert COINTELPRO initiative to destabilize and dissolve perceived subversive groups operating in the United States.

Shakur was wanted for her alleged role in multiple murders and robberies, and was targeted as the leader of a Black Liberation Army cell. In 1973, she was captured and imprisoned after a shootout that resulted in the deaths of her friend Zayd Shakur and New Jersey State Police Trooper Werner Foerster. Shakur was shot twice with her arms raised in surrender. Following multiple lengthy and convoluted trials, Shakur was found guilty for her part in the 1973 shooting, despite evidence that suggesting her innocence. Many believe that her guilt was predetermined by the media frenzy surrounding her fugitive status, which included trumped-up claims and misattributed photographs of other armed African-American women.

Shakur escaped from prison in 1979 with the help of several BLA members, and eventually fled to Cuba. The U.S. government has tried repeatedly to seek extradition from Cuba, and in 2005 the FBI listed Shakur as a "domestic terrorist," offering one million dollars for her capture. Assata Shakur continues to write and speak out against racism from her exile, maintaining her innocence and locating her struggle within the entrenched and institutionalized racism of the United States.

My Mother never
let me forget
my history
Hoping I was set free
chains never
put on me
Wanted to be more
than just free...

Panther power
is running through
my arteries

–Tupac Amaru Shakur

Melanie Cervantes

"They got money for wars but they can't feed the poor."

TUPAC SHAKUR WAS BORN Lesane Parish Crooks in Brooklyn, New York. His mother, Afeni Shakur, was one of the highest ranking women in the New York chapter of the Black Panther Party and changed his name to Tupac Amaru after the revolutionary Incan leader. Shakur grew up in the Bronx and then moved with his mother to Baltimore, where he studied acting at the Baltimore School for the Arts. There, after a friend was shot while playing with guns, he wrote his first rap about gun control and began to perform it. He dropped out of high school (later completing a GED) and moved to northern California with his family.

In 1992, Tupac Shakur was instrumental in getting rival members of the Crips and Bloods to sign the "Code of Thug Life," a lifestyle philosophy and code of conduct created by Shakur and his stepfather Mutulu Shakur. The intention behind the code was to craft principles that encouraged young gangsters to respect and love the communities that they came from. Shakur is often remembered for the social equality messages in his earlier work, and the unique articulation of confusion and rage that characterized his later albums. Shakur's music reflects the complexity of a life spent trying to reconcile a career that brought great fame and riches from a youth of poverty and crime.

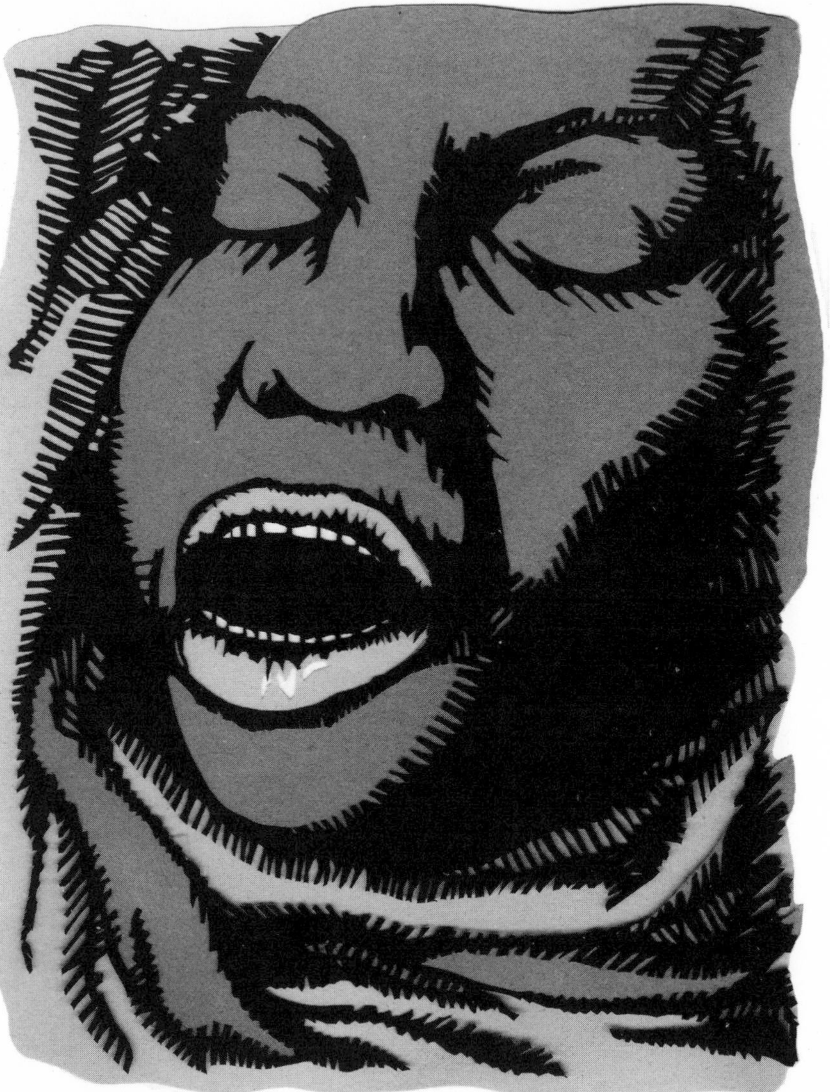

Bec Young

"Slavery has never been abolished from America's way of thinking."

NINA SIMONE WAS BORN Eunice Waymon in rural North Carolina, and began playing the piano at age three. Throughout her youth, Simone encountered continual incidences of racism, which influenced her later involvement in the civil rights movement. During a recital when she was 12 years old, Simone's parents were asked to relinquish their front row seats to a white family, and Simone refused to perform until her parents were returned to their original seats.

After taking a stage name at age 21, to avoid her minister mother knowing she was singing the "devil's music," she began to pursue music as a career. Simone naturally felt inclined towards the burgeoning civil rights movement, and in particular, her friends Lorraine Hansbury and Langston Hughes took steps to educate her and assist her in articulating these issues in her lyrics. In the 1960s, she began to perform songs that openly addressed her experiences with racial inequality in the United States. Simone's songs "Mississippi Goddam" and "Four Women" paint the world as she saw it, laying bare the frustration and anger many people felt at the slow pace of change. Trained as a classical pianist, she truly knew her way around any kind of song, frequently mixing up Broadway styles with jazz and pop tunes. For her multiple talents as a musician and her regal demeanor, Simone earned the title "the High Priestess of Soul." She often performed during important events of the civil rights era, notably during the Selma-to-Montgomery marches in Alabama (1965). Fed up with the racist policies of the United States, Simone spent many of her later years outside of the country. After living in Barbados and Liberia, Simone settled in southern France, where she lived the last 10 years of her life.

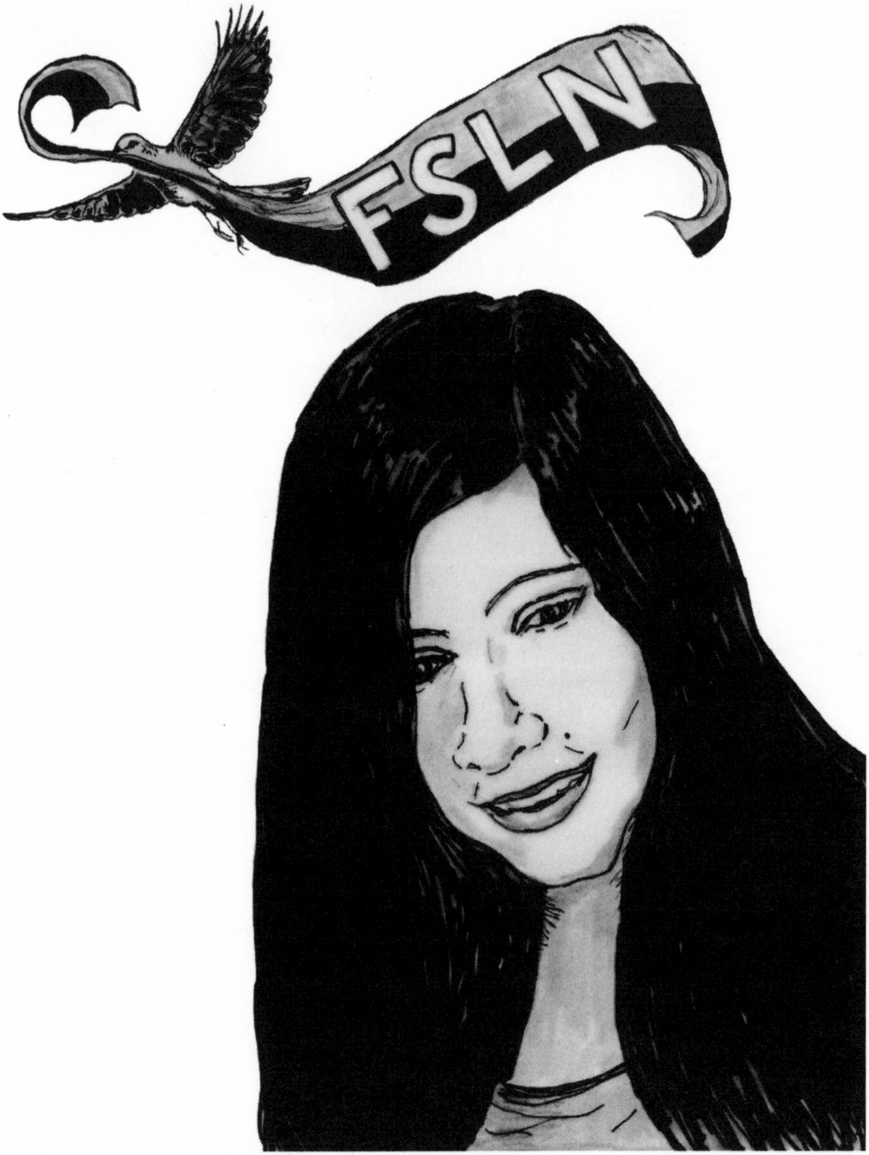
FSLN

Molly Fair

ARLEN SIU BERMÚDEZ WAS born and raised in Jinotepe, Nicaragua. By the time she was in her teens, she was already a celebrated musician, poet and writer. She attended college at the *Nacional Autónoma de Nicaragua* (National Autonomous University of Nicaragua), where she met and performed with the members of the activist music group Pancasán. At age 18, the Chinese-Nicaraguan Siu joined the *Frente Sandinista de Liberación Nacional* (Sandinista National Liberation Front), a political movement of leftist students and peasants attempting to overthrow the Nicaraguan dictator Anastasio Somoza Debayle.

Arlen Siu was dedicated to the Sandinista cause and her music, art and critical essays on Marxism and feminism were an inspiration to the Sandinistas and the Nicaraguan women's movement. On July 31, 1975, Samoza's National Guard attacked a Sandinista training ground in El Sauce, killing Siu and several others. Killed at twenty years of age, she is considered a martyr of the Nicaraguan Revolution. Her song "Maria Rural" is performed by members of Pancasán to this day.

For the footpaths in the fields
you carry the burden of your suffering
the sorrow of your love and your weeping
in your belly of clay and earth...

Malnutrition and poverty
is that which surrounds you
straw huts in silence
only the sound of the forests

Your hands are of cedar
your eyes sadly twilight
your tears are of clay
that spill into the marsh

For this reason on this occasion
today I want to sing to your heart
today I want to tell you what I feel
of too much poverty and desolation

For the prairies and rivers goes the peasant Mother
feeling the cold of winter and her terrible destiny
for the footpaths in fields you carry the burden of
your suffering, the sorrow of your love and weeping
in your belly of clay and earth.

and today I want to sing to you Rural Maria...

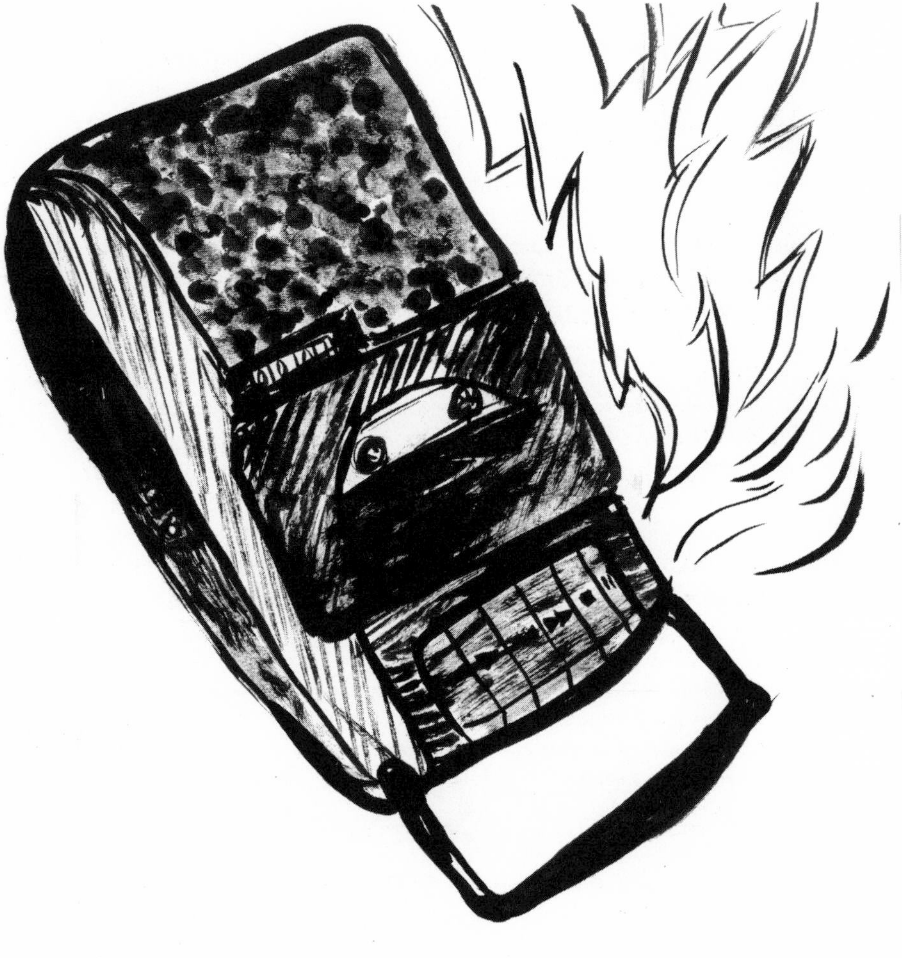

Studs Terkel

{May 16, 1912 - October 31, 2008}

"Take it easy, but take it."

LOUIS "STUDS" TERKEL LEFT behind a life's work of interviews and oral histories of working class Americans. A Pulitzer Prize winner (1985) for his book *The Good War*, Terkel credits his early interest in the stories of everyday people to the Chicago boarding houses his parents ran during his youth. He earned a law degree from the University of Chicago in 1934, but was more interested in acting and throughout the 1940s performed on radio and television programs, including his own radio drama, *Stud's Place*. Terkel was blacklisted in 1953 after investigations by the House Un-American Activities Committee into petitions he had previously signed. Refusing to aid in the persecution of other left-leaning activists, he was banned from radio and television for several years of the "McCarthy Era."

Terkel had a long-running radio show on WFMT in Chicago, originally intended as a space to play music that evolved into a venue to interview all kinds of folks, from performing artists to labor organizers and civil rights activists. These programs constitute an amazing oral documentation of creative personalities, thinkers and most significantly, the lesser-heard voices of Americans from all walks of life. Well-known for his mastery of the interview, Studs Terkel let people talk about what they knew best. He also authored many books collecting transcriptions of his conversations. Terkel advocated for social justice and openly criticized the U.S. government's abuse of authority. In 2006, he joined a suit seeking to block AT&T and other phone companies from giving customer records to the National Security Agency without a warrant. He survived open-heart surgery at age 93.

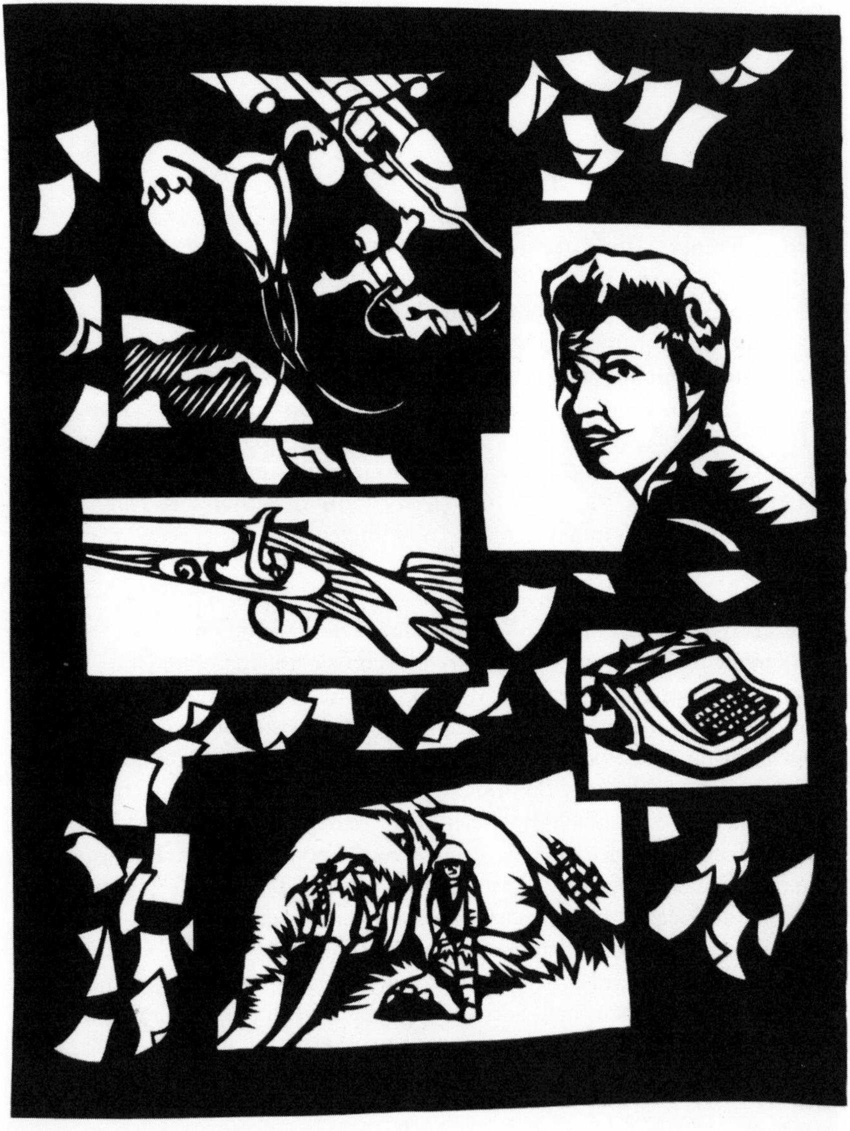

"I don't identify with 'normality', not in this world."

JAMES TIPTREE JR. REVOLUTIONIZED American science fiction in the 1960s with a series of incredibly powerful short stories. His evocations of sex, death and strangeness shattered contemporary perceptions of what speculative fiction could accomplish, and were all the more impressive for the strict feminism that seemed to inform them. It was a revolutionary thing for a man to write so powerfully and insightfully about the condition of women in a society dominated by men. His stories detonated within the genre for more than 10 years, inspiring a generation of young writers.

In 1976, the field of science fiction was shocked again; James Tiptree Jr. was actually a woman named Alice Bradley Sheldon. As a child, Sheldon was taken along by her novelist-explorer parents on expeditions to parts of Africa where whites had never previously been seen. She spent her youth as an artist and critic, before enlisting in the army, working for an early incarnation of the CIA and earning a Ph.D. in psychology. When she began to write her pointedly feminist fictions, she took up a male pen name for fun. The Tiptree persona became an emblem for feminist writers and thinkers throughout the tumultuous 60s and 70s, who pointed to his stories as evidence that men could learn to see the world through women's eyes. The eventual discovery of the persona only added further nuance to the debate, and further power to the Tiptree stories. Sheldon continued to write fiction and to carry on influential correspondence with writers of the day. She struggled to speak truthfully and unflinchingly about the human condition and the dire state of affairs that humans have created here on Earth. She killed herself and her ailing husband with a revolver in 1987.

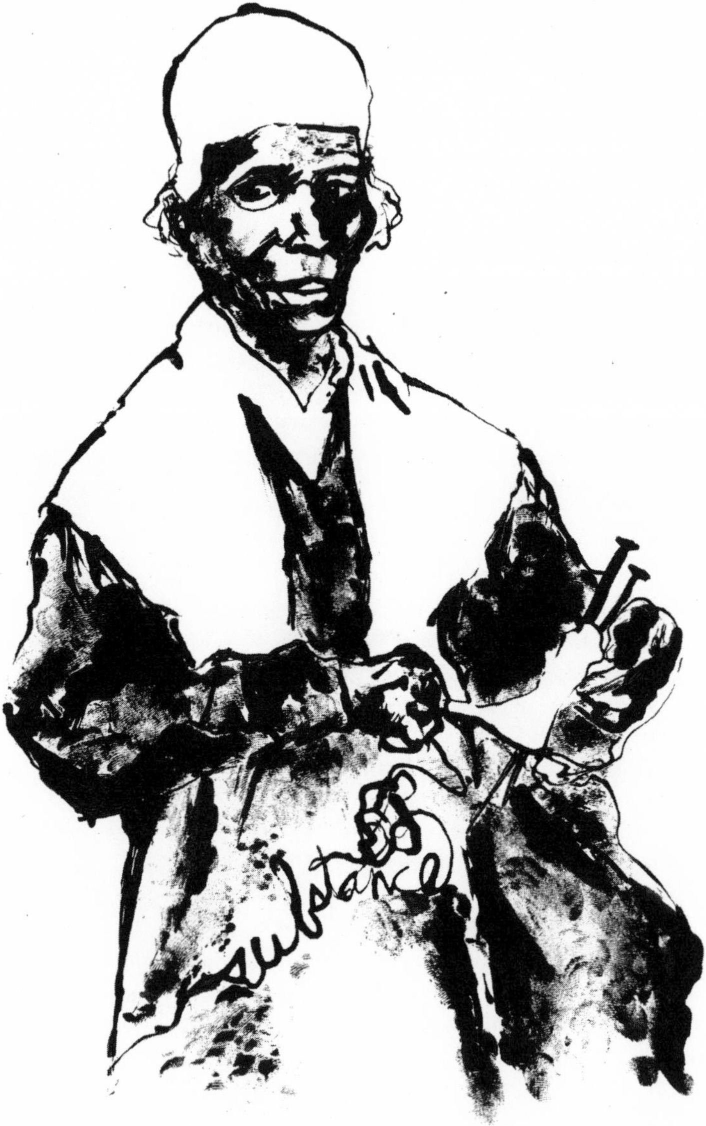
substance

Mary Tremonte

Sojourner Truth

{1797 - NOVEMBER 26, 1883}

ISABELLA BAUMFREE WAS BORN a slave to Dutch owners in upstate New York, and sold several times to different men throughout her young adult life. Her first love, a slave named Roger, was severely beaten by his master for his affair with a woman who belonged to another slave-owner. She had five children (one by Roger) and was eventually estranged from most of them through the morass of emancipation laws in the pre-abolition North. In 1827, she used the judicial system to rescue her son Peter from an Alabama plantation where he had been sold off illegally when he was five.

After a personal spiritual awakening in 1843, Baumfree changed her name to Sojourner Truth and set upon her new calling as an itinerant preacher. Wandering in relative obscurity, she depended on the kindness of strangers. Truth spent some years involved in the utopian communities of the Kingdom of Matthias and the Northampton Association of Education and Industry. In 1858, at a Spiritualist meeting in Silver Lake, Indiana, someone in the audience accused the particularly tall Sojourner Truth of being a man, and she opened her blouse to reveal her breasts to the crowd. In her later life, she campaigned with little success for the federal government to provide former slaves with land in the "new West," and continued to work in the west helping refugee slaves start their new lives.

Truth did not read or write; consequentially her words have been filtered through the hands of those who did, with sometimes different motivations. A staunch feminist and abolitionist, her narrative holds a unique place in American history. As the legacy of an emancipated slave from the North, rather than the Southeast, Truth's story serves as a reminder of the wide scope and impact of slavery in the United States.

Chris Stain

Denmark Vesey

{CA.1767 - CA.1822}

BORN TELEMANQUE AND LATER named Denmark Vesey by his master, Vesey was an educated Caribbean slave who bought his freedom with a portion of the 1,500 dollars he won from a lottery in 1800. A skilled carpenter and sailor, Vesey was known for reading aloud both the Bible and insurrectionary pamphlets smuggled into South Carolina by other sailors. He was implicated and quickly executed as a lead conspirator in an alleged uprising, expected to take place in the summer of 1822. In the plan, the city of Charleston was to be overtaken, through the cooperation of thousands of slaves and others, spanning nationality and trade; the insurrection would have been enormous in scale.

Vesey and 34 others were hung, with many more arrested on conspiracy charges. However, contemporary evidence suggests that the round up, interrogation and execution of Vesey and dozens of other slaves and free men was likely a witch-hunt orchestrated by local politicians and judges, preying on Southern white fears of an armed revolution of righteously angry slaves. Little evidence exists of the actuality of a plot other than court documentation, which indicates heavy witness intimidation, torture and a lack of due process in the trials. Many of those arrested gave elaborate, and often conflicting, testimonies. For his part, Vesey maintained his innocence all the way to the gallows.

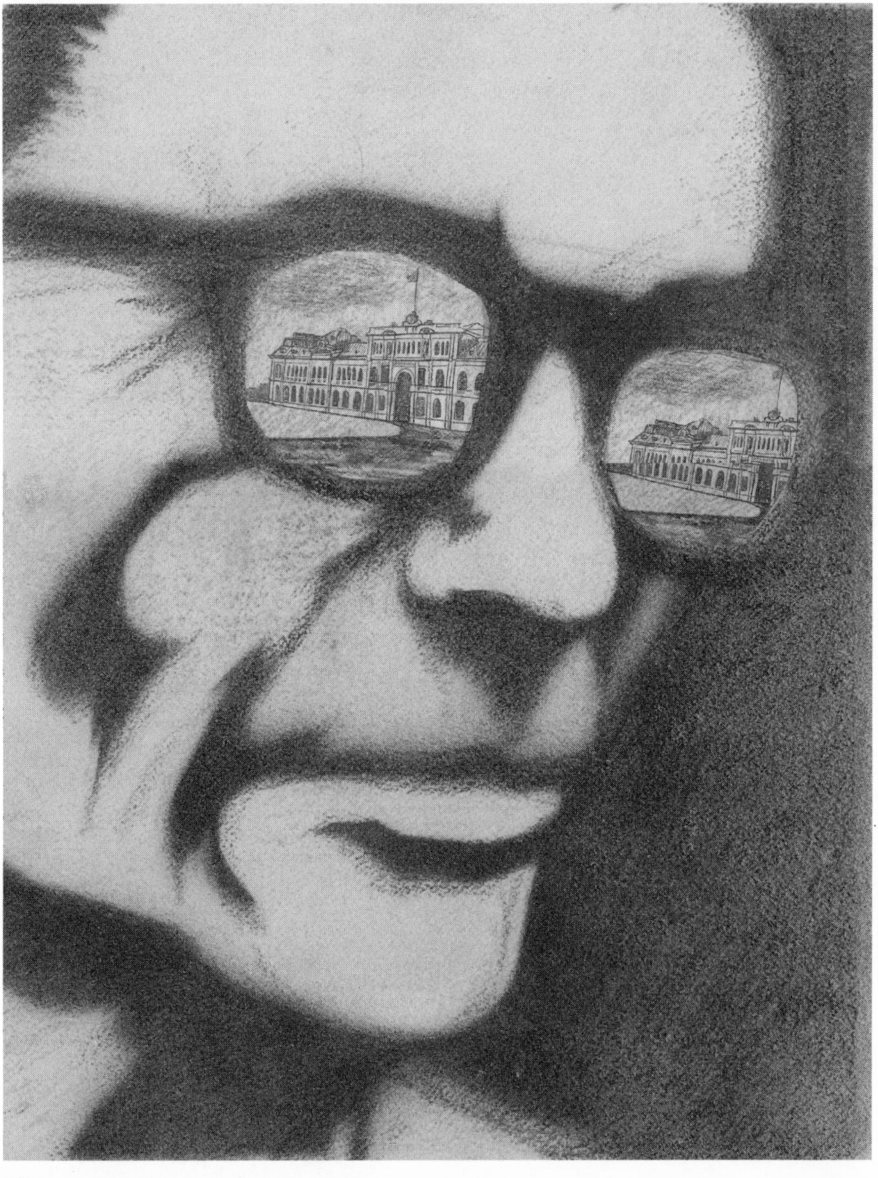

Bec Young

Rodolfo Walsh

"Nothing can stop us, neither jail nor death. Because you can't jail or kill a whole people and because the vast majority of Argentinians…know that only the people will save the people."

RODOLFO WALSH WAS BORN in the Patagonia region of Argentina and descended from Irish immigrants who escaped the potato famine. He worked from a young age in the newspaper business, became a journalist and later a writer of detective stories. His 1957 account of the brutal treatment of Peronist rebels, *Operación Massacre*, is considered to be the first political testimonial in Latin America and the first example of investigative journalism published as a novel. Walsh went to Cuba after the revolution, and in 1959 set up the *Prensa Libre*, the press agency of the revolution, with other Argentine activists. While in Cuba, he deciphered a telex code using an old book of cryptography, alerting the Cubans to the 1961 "Bay of Pigs Invasion," a failed, U.S.-backed attempt at government overthrow.

Although he was part of the infamous Peronist guerilla group, the Montoneros, he grew to disagree with some of their more violent tactics, and wrote about it in a series of essays now known as *The Walsh Papers*. At the time of the 1976 coup in Argentina, Walsh had been running a clandestine news agency called ANCLA. Walsh was also heartbroken by the death of his daughter, herself a Montonero guerilla, that same year. On March 24, 1977, Walsh printed and distributed his "Open Letter From a Writer to the Military Junta," not only railing against the physical violence, but the economic policies he argued would lead millions of Argentines into "planned misery" long after the dictatorship was over. Hours after he delivered the letter, Walsh was "disappeared" by the military and was never seen again.

Yours for Justice,
IDA B. WELLS

Nicolas Lampert

Ida B. Wells-Barnett

"One had better die fighting against injustice than die like a dog or a rat in a trap."

THE STATEMENT WITH WHICH Ida B. Wells closed her correspondence, "Yours for Justice," epitomizes how she lived and the legacy she left behind. Wells was a tireless anti-lynching crusader, a suffragist, a women's rights advocate, a journalist and speaker. She was born in 1862 in Holly Springs, Mississippi and moved to Memphis in 1880. There, she began her career as a journalist, writing editorials about race relations in the U.S. for the *Evening Star* and the *Living Way*. In 1889, she became co-owner and editor of the anti-segregationist newspaper *Free Speech*.

Well's confrontational journalism gained her immediate notoriety. After the open lynching of three of Well's friends in 1892, she recommended that African-American residents move away from Memphis, and her statements left her own safety compromised. She relocated to Philadelphia and eventually settled in Chicago. There she continued to advocate against lynching, and wrote a book, *Southern Horrors: Lynch Law in All Its Phases*. Wells married Ferdinand L. Barnett, became active in the women's suffrage movement, helped organize African-American women in her community and rallied against the racism that was active within the national suffragist movement. She helped lay the groundwork for the formation of the Niagara Movement and the NAACP and was one of the first African-American women to run for public office in the U.S., in an unsuccessful bid for a seat on the Illinois Legislature.

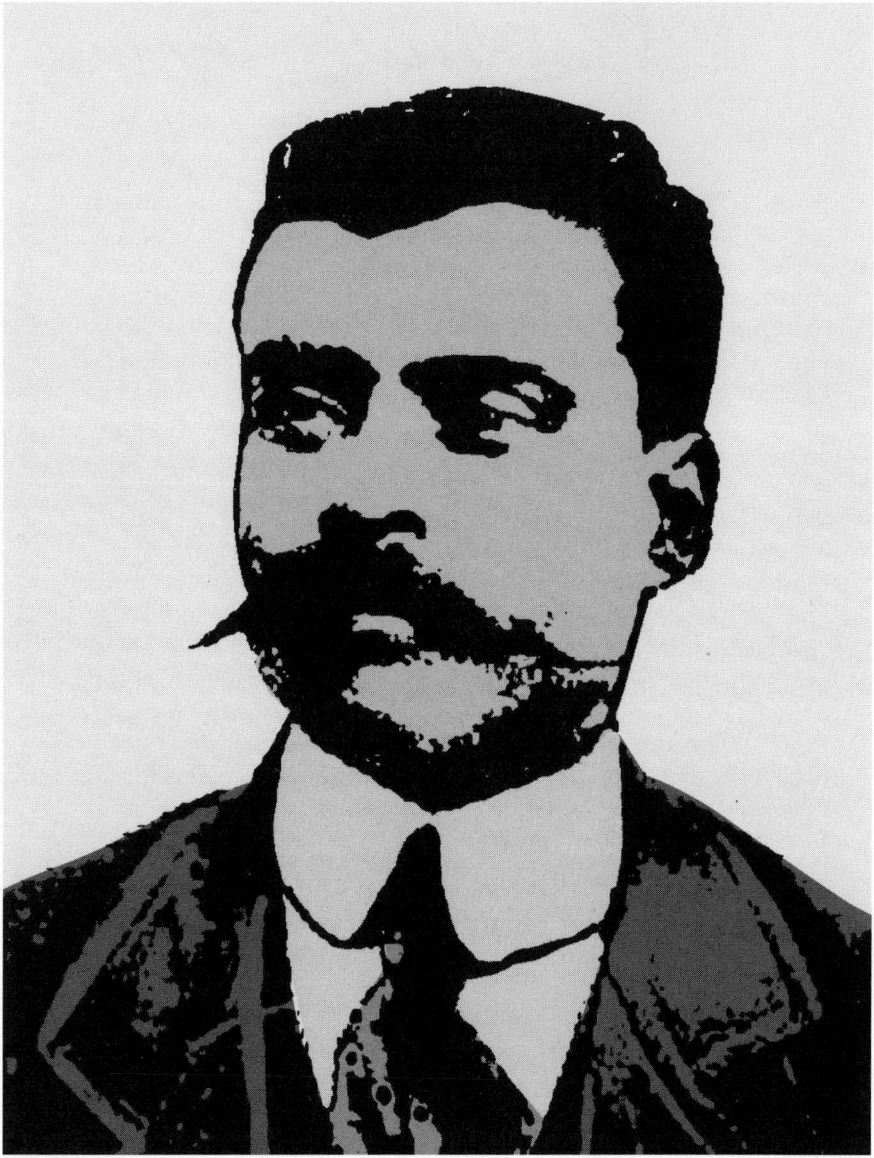

Jesus Barraza

Emiliano Zapata

"The land belongs to those that work it."

{August 8, 1879 - April 10, 1919}

BY 30 YEARS OF age, Emiliano Zapata had become a council president of Anenecuilco, his community in Mexico, where he was part of the struggle for farm workers' rights. In 1910 he became a general in the Mexican Revolution. Leading forces from the south of Mexico alongside Pancho Villa's forces from the north, among others, he helped to overthrow President Porfirio Diaz with the hopes of agrarian reform. Zapata continued to fight subsequent leaders who failed to effect fundamental changes he believed in. He helped author the *Plan de Ayala*, which called for the transfer of land from *hacendados* (owners of large estates or plantations) to townships and citizens and upheld the nativist, agrarian roots of the revolution.

Emiliano Zapata was not only a military leader and visionary, but a symbol of the open expression of class struggle at the root of the movement for national liberation. After nearly a decade of battling dictatorships, he was murdered in an ambush in 1919. In 1994, the *Ejército Zapatista de Liberacion Naciònal* (Zapatista Army for National Liberation) made its existence known to the world, with the call of *"¡Basta Ya!"* (Enough Already!) and *"Tierra y Libertad"* (Land and Liberty), taking Zapata's understanding, that the people who work the land should own the land, as part of their militant worldview.

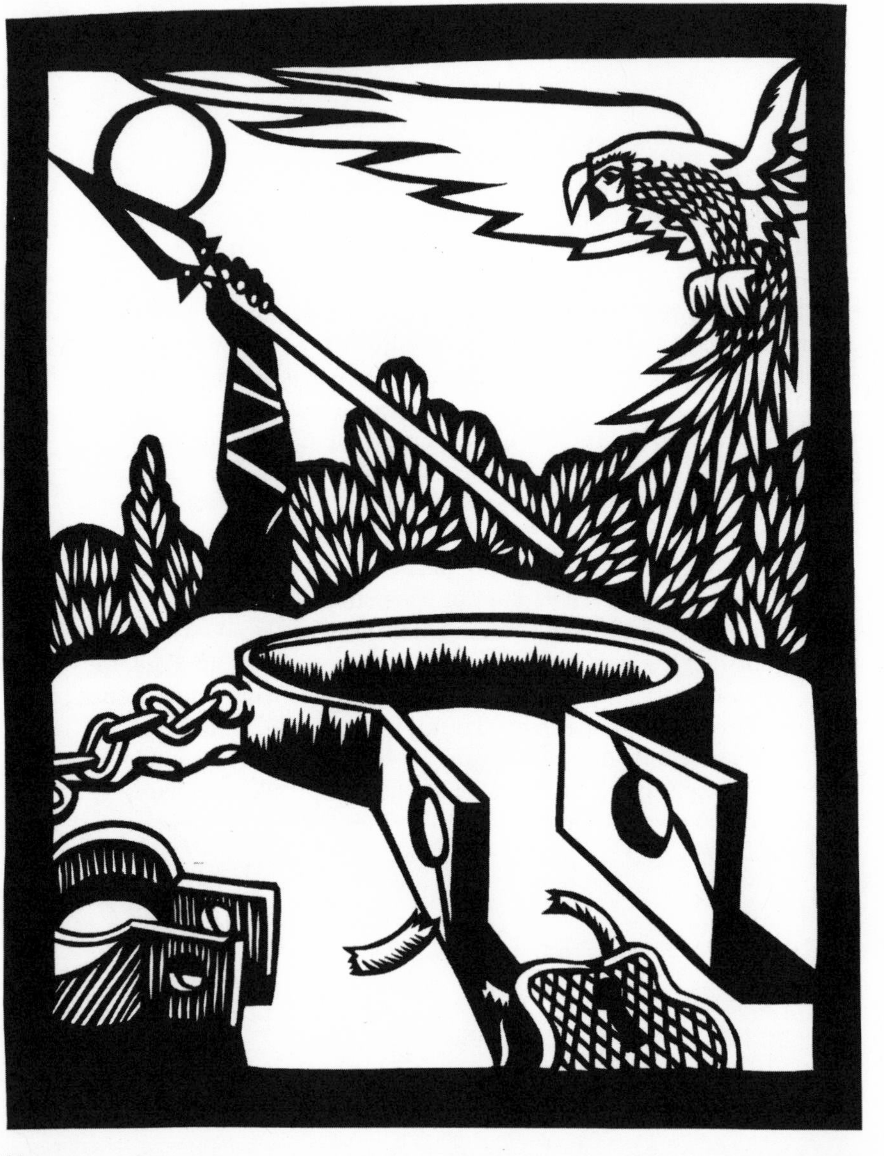

Roger Peet

Zumbi dos Palmares

"I don't believe in the word of my enemies. My enemies don't believe it themselves."

THE SLAVES OF BRAZIL were always a rebellious group. Stolen from the western coast of Africa, they were forced into labor on vast plantations of sugar cane. They were beaten and herded like cattle by overseers, and developed a habit of escaping to set up free enclaves in the endless forests. These communities came to be known as *quilombos*, and they continued to be a thorn in the side of colonial administrations for decades. The largest was Palmares, which at its height boasted a population in the tens of thousands. They were a people drawn from multitudes of African tribes, *mestizos* and Indians. Expeditions sent by the ruling Portuguese claimed occasional prisoners, but the temptation Palmares presented to slaves ensured a constant stream of new arrivals.

The Portuguese made an offer to the king of Palmares, Ganga Zumba, in 1678: Dissolve your community, and we will give you freedom. You will be richly rewarded. Bring your people from the jungle down to the plains, and everyone born in Palmares can go free. The escaped slaves, however, must be returned to us. Ganga Zumba wearily agreed. Only five thousand of the 30 thousand residents of Palmares accompanied him. The rest stayed on under Zumbi, Ganga Zumba's nephew. Zumbi vowed to stay, and the people of Palmares stayed with him. They turned to face the winds of war.

Sixteen years later the Portuguese sent a final expedition to Palmares, nine thousand men with cannons slogging through the jungle. They attacked Macacos, the capital of Palmares, and tore it to the ground. The communities were burned and the residents scattered. Zumbi escaped, only to be betrayed and murdered a year later. Zumbi lent his name to the leaders of many successive slave rebellions, and is considered the patron saint of the Brazilian fighting art, Capoeira.

MUHAMMAD ALI
Muhammad Ali Handbook, Dave Zirin, MQ Publications, Ltd, 2007.
A People's History of Sports in the United States, Dave Zirin, The New Press, 2008.
What's My Name Fool? Sports and Resistance in the United States, Dave Zirin,
   Haymarket Books, 2005.

GLORIA ANZALDÚA
Borderlands/La Frontera: The New Mestiza, Gloria Anzaldúa, Aunt Lute, 1987.
Interviews/Entrevistas, edited by AnaLouise Keating, Routledge, 2000.

KUWASI BALAGOON
A Soldier's Story: Writings By A Revolutionary New Afrikan Anarchist, Kuwasi
   Balagoon, Kersplebedeb, 2001.
Look for Me in the Whirlwind: The Collective Autobiography of the New York 21,
   Kuwasi Balagoon, et al., Random House, 1971.

JUDI BARI
Timber Wars, Judi Bari, Common Courage Press, 1994.

RAFAEL BARRETT
Asombro y búsqueda de Rafael Barrett, Gregorio Morán, Editorial Anagrama, 2007
   (in Spanish).

DOMITILA BARRIOS DE CHUNGARA
Let Me Speak! Testimony of Domitila, A Woman of the Bolivian Mines, Domitila
   Barrios de Chungara, Monthly Review Press, 1979.
*Women Imagine Change: A Global Anthology of Women's Resistance from 600 B.C.E.
   to Present,* edited by Eugenia Delamotte, Routledge, 1997.

GRACE LEE BOGGS
Living for Change: An Autobiography, Grace Lee Boggs, University of Minnesota
   Press, 1998.
Revolution and Evolution in the Twentieth Century, James Boggs and Grace Lee
   Boggs, Monthly Review Press, 1974.

SIMÓN BOLIVAR
Simón Bolivar: A Life, John Lynch, Yale University Press, 2007.
El Libertador: Writings of Simón Bolivar, Simón Bolivar, Oxford Univ. Press, 2003.

JOHN BROWN
*John Brown, Abolitionist : The Man Who Killed Slavery, Sparked the Civil War,
   and Seeded Civil Rights,* David S. Reynolds, Vintage, 2005.

John Brown, W.E.B. Du Bois, Modern Library, 2001 (orig. 1974).
Cloudsplitter: A Novel, Russell Banks, Harper Perennial, 1998.

SITTING BULL
Sitting Bull, Bill Yenne, Westholme Publishing, 2008.
The Ghost-Dance Religion and the Sioux Outbreak of 1890, James Mooney,
    University of Nebraska, 1991 (orig. 1896).

LUISA CAPETILLO
A Nation of Women: An Early Feminist Speaks Out, Luisa Capetillo, Arte
    Publico Press, 2004.
Luisa Capetillo: Pasión de Justicia (film) dir. Sonia Fritz, 1995.
Luisa Capetillo, Pioneer Puerto Rican Feminist, Norma Valle-Ferrer, Peter Lang
    Publishing, 2006

RACHEL CARSON
Silent Spring, Rachel Carson, Houghton Mifflin, 1962.
Rachel Carson: Witness for Nature, Linda Lear, Henry Holt, 1997.
The Sense of Wonder, Rachel Carson, Harper Collins, 1998 (orig. 1965).

BARTOLOMÉ DE LAS CASAS
A Short Account of the Destruction of the Indies, Bartolomé de las Casas,
    Penguin Classics, 1999.
Bartolomé de Las Casas: Great Prophet of the Americas, Paul S. Vickery,
    The Newman Press, 2006.

ELIZABETH CATLETT
Elizabeth Catlett: In the Image of the People, Melanie Anne Herzog, Art
    Institute of Chicago, 2005

ROBERTO CLEMENTE
A Peoples History of Sports in the United States, Dave Zirin, The New Press, 2008.
Clemente: the Passion and Grace of Baseball's Last Hero, David Maraniss, Simon
    and Schuster, 2006.
Welcome to the Terrordome, Dave Zirin, Haymarket Books, 2007.

CARLOS CORTÉZ
Where Are The Voices? & Other Wobbly Poems, Carlos Cortéz, Charles H.
    Kerr, 1997.
*Yours for the OBU: Radical Wobbly Traditions in the Art of Carlos Cortéz
    Koyokuikatl and Dylan A.T. Miner,* Dylan Miner, ed., Amoxtli Press,
    2005.

Carlos Cortéz Koyokuikatl: Soapbox Artist & Poet, Victor Alejandro Sorrell &
    Robert L. Weitz, Mexican Fine Arts Center Museum , 2001.

ROQUE DALTON
Clandestine Poems / Poemas Clandestinos, Roque Dalton, Curbstone Press, 1990.
Small Hours of the Night, Roque Dalton, Curbstone Press, 1997.
Miguel Mármol: A Testimony, Roque Dalton, Curbstone Press, 1987.

JUSTIN DART
Disabled Rights: American Disability Policy and the Fight for Equality, Jacqueline
    Vaughn, Georgetown University Press, 2003.
Enabling Lives: Biographies of Six Prominent Americans with Disabilities, Brian T
    McMahon and Linda R Shaw, CRC Press, 2000.

ANGELA DAVIS
Angela Davis: An Autobiography, Angela Y. Davis, International Publishers, 1989
Women, Race, & Class, Angela Davis, Vintage, 1983 (orig. 1981).
The Angela Y. Davis Reader, Angela Y. Davis & Joy James (editor), Blackwell
    Publishing, 1998.

DOROTHY DAY
Dorothy Day: A Radical Devotion, Robert Coles, Persueus Books, 1989.
Loaves and Fishes, Dorothy Day, Orbis Books, 1997 (orig. 1983).

VOLTAIRINE DE CLEYRE
The Voltairine de Cleyre Reader, Voltairine de Cleyre (ed. by A.J. Brigati), AK
    Press, 2004.
An American Anarchist: The Life of Voltairine de Cleyre, Paul Avrich, Princeton
    University Press, 1978.

EUGENE DEBS
Debs: His Life, Writings and Speeches, Eugene V. Debs, University Press of the
    Pacific, 2002.
The Bending Cross: A Biography of Eugene Victor Debs, Ray Ginger, Haymarket
    Books, 2007 (first pub. 1949).
Walls & Bars: Prisons & Prison Life In The "Land Of The Free", Eugene V. Debs,
    Charles H. Kerr, 1983 (first pub. 1927).

W.E.B. DU BOIS
The Souls of Black Folk, W.E.B. Du Bois, Penguin Classics, 1996 (orig. 1903).
W.E.B. Du Bois: Biography of a Race, David Levering Lewis, Topeka Bindery, 2003.

FRANTZ FANON
The Wretched of the Earth, Frantz Fanon, Grove Press, 2004.
Black Skin, White Masks, Frantz Fanon, Grove Press, 1967.
Frantz Fanon: A Biography, David Macey, Picador Press, 2000.

URSULA MARTIUS FRANKLIN
The Ursula Franklin Reader: Pacifism as a Map, Ursula Franklin, Between the
   Lines, 2006.

PAULO FREIRE
Pedagogy of the Oppressed, Paulo Freire, Continuum International Press, 2000
   (orig. 1967).
Pedagogy of Hope, Paulo Freire, Continuum International Press, 2004
   (orig. 1994).

R. BUCKMINSTER FULLER
Critical Path, R. Buckminster Fuller, St. Martin's Griffin, 1982.
Operating Manual for Spaceship Earth, R. Buckminster Fuller, Amereon Limited,
   1978 (orig. 1969).
I Seem to Be a Verb, R. Buckminster Fuller w/ Quentin Fiore & Jerome Agel,
   Bantam Books, 1970.

GERONIMO
Bury My Heart at Wounded Knee, Dee Brown, Owl Books, 2001 (orig. 1970).
Once They Moved Like The Wind : Cochise, Geronimo, And The Apache Wars, David
   Roberts, Touchstone, 1993.

EMMA GOLDMAN
Living My Life, Emma Goldman, Courier Dover Publications,1970 (orig. 1931).
A Dangerous Woman, Sharon Rudahl, The New Press, 2007.
Anarchism and Other Essays, Emma Goldman, Dover, 1969 (orig. 1910).

ALBERT "GINGER" GOODWIN
Fighting for Dignity: The Ginger Goodwin Story, Roger Stonebanks, Canadian
   Committee on Labour History, 2004.
Ginger: The Life and Death of Albert Goodwin, Susan Mayse, Harbour, 1990.

SARAH & ANGELINA GRIMKE
The Grimke Sisters From South Carolina, Rebels Against Slavery, Gerda Lerner,
   University of North Carolina Press, 2004.
*Lift Up Thy Voice, The Grimke Family's Journey from Slaveholders to Civil Rights
   Leaders,* Mark Perry, Penguin, 2002.

ELIZABETH GURLEY FLYNN

Words on Fire: The Life and Writing of Elizabeth Gurley Flynn , Rosalyn Baxandall,
    Rutgers University Press, 1987.
*The Rebel Girl, An Autobiography, My First Life (1906-1926)***,** Elizabeth Gurley
    Flynn, International Publishers, 1955.
The Alderson Story: My Life As a Political Prisoner, Elizabeth Gurley Flynn,
    International Publishers, 1963.

WOODY GUTHRIE

Bound for Glory, Woody Guthrie, Plume, 1983 (orig. 1969).
Pastures of Plenty: A Self-Portrait, Woody Guthrie, Perrenial, 1992.
Woody Guthrie: A Life, Joe Klein, Delta, 1999 (orig. 1980).

FRED HAMPTON

*The Assassination of Fred Hampton: How the FBI and the Chicago Police Murdered a
    Black Panther,* Jeffrey Haas, Lawrence Hill Books, 2009.
The Murder of Fred Hampton, (documentary film) Mike Gray & Howard Alk,
    1971.
The Cointelpro Papers, Ward Churchill & Fred Vander Wall, South End Press, 2001.

HATUEY

Cuba: A New History, Richard Gott, Yale University, 2004.

"BIG BILL" HAYWOOD

Roughneck: The Life and Times of Big Bill Haywood, Peter Carlson,
    W. W. Norton, 1983.
Big Bill: Haywood, Melvyn Dubofsky, St. Martin's Press, 1987.
Wobblies! A Graphic History of the Industrial Workers of the World, edited by Paul
    Buhle, Verso, 2005.

C.L.R. JAMES

C.L.R. James: The Artist as Revolutionary, Paul Buhle, Verso, 1989.
Beyond a Boundary, C.L.R. James, Yellow Jersey Press, 1994.

FRIDA KAHLO

Devouring Frida: The Art History and Popular Celebrity of Frida Kahlo, Margaret A.
    Lindauer, Wesleyan University Press, 1999
The Diary of Frida Kahlo: An Intimate Self-Portrait, Frida Kahlo, Carlos Fuentes
    and Sarah. M Lowe, Harry N. Abrams, Inc, 2005 (orig. 1995)

HELEN KELLER

Helen Keller: Selected Writings, Helen Keller, New York University Press, 2005.

The Radical Lives of Helen Keller, Kim Nielson, New York University Press, 2004.
Helen Keller, A Life, Dorothy Herrmann, University of Chicago Press, 1999.

FLORYNCE KENNEDY
Color Me Flo: My Hard Life and Good Times, Florynce Kennedy, Prentice Hall,1976.

YURI KOCHIYAMA
Passing It On, Yuri Kochiyama, UCLA Asian-American Studies Center Press, 2004.
Yuri Kochiyama: Heartbeat of a Struggle, Diane Fujino, Univ. of Minnesota Press, 2005.
Yuri Kochiyama: Passion for Justice (documentary film), Rea Tajiri, 1999.

TOUSSAINT L'OUVERTURE
The Black Jacobins: Toussaint L'Ouverture and the San Domingo Revolution, C.L.R. James, Vintage, 1989 (orig. 1939).

LILI'UOKALANI
Notes from a Native Daughter: Colonialism and Sovereignty in Hawai'i, Haunani-Kay Trask, University of Hawai'i, 1999 (2nd edition).
Aloha Betrayed: Native Hawaiian Resistance to American Colonialism, Noenoe Silva, Duke University Press, 2004.

AUDRE LORDE
Zami: A New Spelling of My Name, Audre Lorde, Crossing Press, 1982.
Sister Outsider: Essays and Speeches, Audre Lorde, Crossing Press, 1984.
Warrior Poet: A Biography of Audre Lorde, Alexis De Veaux, W.W. Norton, 2006.

JOSÉ MARTÍ
The José Martí Reader: Writings on the Americas, José Martí, Ocean Press 2006 (orig. 1999).
Come, Come - My Boiling Blood, The Complete Poems of José Martí, trans. Jack Agueros, Curbstone Press, 2007.

RICARDO FLORES MAGÓN
Dreams of Freedom: A Ricardo Flores Magón Reader, Ricardo Flores Magón, AK Press, 2005.
Anarchism and the Mexican Revolution, Colin M. MacLachan, University of California Press, 1991.
Always a Rebel, Ward S. Albro, Texas Christian University Press, 1992.

ELIZABETH "BETITA" MARTINEZ

Letters from Mississippi: Reports from Civil Rights Volunteers and Freedom School Poetry of the 1964 Freedom Summer, edited by Elizabeth Betita Martinez, Zephyr, 2007.

500 Años Del Pueblo Chicano / 500 Years of Chicano History: In Pictures, Elizabeth Betita Martinez, Southwest Organizing Project, 1990.

De Colores Means All of Us: Latina Views for a Multi-Colored Century, Elizabeth Betita Martínez, South End Press, 1998.

RIGOBERTA MENCHÚ

I, Rigoberta Menchú: An Indian Woman in Guatemala, Rigoberta Menchú, Verso, 1987.

Crossing Borders, Rigoberta Menchú, Verso, 1998.

CHICO MENDES

The Burning Season, Andrew Revkin, Hougton Mifflin, 1990.

ALICIA MOREAU DE JUSTO

Century of the Wind, Memory of Fire #3, Eduardo Galeano, W.W. Norton & Company, 1998 (orig.1986).

HENRY MORGENTALER

Morgentaler: A Difficult Hero, Catherine Dunphy, Random House Canada, 1996.

Morgentaler: The Doctor Who Couldn't Turn Away, Eleanor Wright Pelrine, Goodread Biographies, 1983.

NANNY OF THE MAROONS

The Mother of Us All: A History of Queen Nanny, Leader of the Windward Jamaican Maroons, Karla Gottlieb, Africa World Press, 2000

Black Rebels: African Caribbean Freedom Fighters in Jamaica, Werner Zips, Marcus Wiener, 1999.

Maroon Societies: Rebel Slave Communities in the Americas, Richard Price, John Hopkins University, 1996.

PABLO NERUDA

The Essential Neruda, edited by Mark Eisner, City Lights, 2004.

Neruda: An Intimate Biography, Volodia Teitelbom, University Of Texas Press, 1991.

Verses Against the Darkness: Pablo Neruda's Poetry and Politics, Greg Dawes, Bucknell University Press, 2006.

Memoirs, Pablo Neruda, Farrar, Straus and Giroux, 1974.

GRACE PALEY

Grace Paley's Life Stories, Judith Arcana, University of Illinois Press, 1993.

Collected Stories, Grace Paley, Farrar, Straus & Giroux, 1994.
Begin Again: Collected Poems, Grace Paley, Farrar, Straus & Giroux, 2000.
Just As I Thought, Grace Paley, Farrar, Straus & Giroux, 1998.

Po'pay

Indian Uprising on the Rio Grande: The Pueblo Revolt of 1680, Franklin Folsom,
    University of New Mexico, 1996.
Pueblo Profiles: Cultural Identity through Centuries of Change, Joe Sando, Clear Light, 1998.
Po'pay: Leader of the First American Revolution, Joe Sando and Herman Agoyo,
    Clear Light, 2005.
The Pueblo Revolt: The Secret Rebellion that Drove the Spaniards Out of the Southwest,
    David Roberts, Simon & Schuster, 2004.

Comandante Ramona

The Zapatista Reader, Tom Hayden, Thunder's Mouth Press, 2001.
Homage to Chiapas: The New Indigenous Struggles in Mexico, Bill Weinberg,
    Verso, 2002.

Louis Riel

Louis Riel: A Comic-Strip Biography, Chester Brown, Drawn and Quarterly, 2003.
Prison of Grass: Canada from a Native Point of View, Howard Adams, Fifth House,
    1989 (orig. 1975).
Louis Riel, Joanne Pelletier, Gabriel Dumont Institute, 1985.

Marlon Riggs

Out in Culture: Gay, Lesbian, and Queer Essays on Popular Culture, Edited by Corey
    K. Creekmur and Alexander Doty, Duke University Press, 1995.
I Shall Not Be Removed: The Life of Marlon Riggs (dir. Karen Everett, 1996)
Films by Riggs: *Black is Black Ain't (1995), Color Adjustment (1992), Non, Je Ne
    Regrette Rien (No Regret) (1992), Anthem (1991), Affirmations (1990), Tongues
    Untied (1989), Ethnic Notions (1987).*

Sylvia Rivera

Trans Liberation: Beyond Pink or Blue, Leslie Feinberg, Beacon, 1998.
Stonewall, Martin Duberman, Plume, 1994.
Fenced Out, Paper Tiger, video #304, 2001.

Paul Robeson

Here I Stand, Paul Robeson, Beacon Press, 1998.
Paul Robeson: A Biography, Martin B. Duberman, The New Press, 2007.

WALTER RODNEY
How Europe Underdeveloped Africa, Walter Rodney, Howard University Press, 1981.
The Groundings With My Brothers, Walter Rodney, Bogle-L'Ouverture
    Publications Ltd., 1969.
Walter Rodney Speaks: the Making of an African Intellectual, edited by Robert A.
    Hill, Africa World Press, 1990.

NICOLA SACCO AND BARTOLOMEO VANZETTI
Sacco and Vanzetti: The Anarchist Background, Paul Avrich, Princeton Univiverstiy
    Press, 1996.
Sacco and Vanzetti: The Men, The Murders, and the Judgment of Mankind, Bruce
    Watson, Viking, 2007.
Sacco and Vanzetti: Rebel Lives, Ferdinando Nicola Sacco and Bartolomeo
    Vanzetti (ed. by John Davis), Ocean Press, 2004.

AUGUSTO CÉSAR SANDINO
The Sandino Affair, Neill Macaulay, Duke University Press, 1985.
Sandino's Daughters: Testimonies of Nicaraguan Women in Struggle, Margaret Randall,
    Rutgers University Press, 1995.

ASSATA SHAKUR
Assata: An Autobiography, Assata Shakur, Lawrence Hill, 1999 (orig. 1987).
Still Black, Still Strong, Dhoruba BinWahad, Assata Shakur and Mumia Abu-
    Jamal, Semiotext(e), 1993.

TUPAC SHAKUR
Tupac Shakur: Legacy, Jamal Joseph, Atria, 2006.
The Rose that Grew from Concrete, Tupac Shakur, MTV, 1999.

NINA SIMONE
I Put a Spell On You: Autobiography of Nina Simone, Nina Simone, Da Capo Press,
    1993.

ARLEN SIU
Encounters: People of Asian Descent in the Americas, Roshni Rustomji-Kerns, Rajini
    Srikanth, Leny Mendoza Strobel (eds.), Rowman & Littlefield, 1999.
Nicaragua: June 1978 - July 1979, Susan Meiselas, Claire Rosenberg, Aperture,
    2008.

STUDS TERKEL
*Working: People Talk About What They Do All Day and How They Feel About What
    They Do,* Studs Terkel, New Press, 1997 (orig. 1974).

The Studs Terkel Reader: My American Century, Studs Terkel, New Press, 2007 (orig. 1997).
Race: What Blacks and Whites Think and Feel About the American Obsession, Studs Terkel, New Press, 2005.
The Good War, Studs Terkel, New Press, 1997.

JAMES TIPTREE, JR.
Her Smoke Rose Up Forever, James Tiptree, Jr., Tachyon Publications, 2004 (orig. 1990).
James Tiptree, Jr.: The Double Life of Alice B. Sheldon, Julie Phillips, St. Martin's Press, 2006.

SOJOURNER TRUTH
Narrative of Sojourner Truth, Sojourner Truth, Dover, 1993 (orig. 1850).
Sojourner Truth: A Life, a Symbol, Nell Irvin Painter, W.W. Norton, 1997.

DENMARK VESEY
Denmark Vesey: The Buried Story of America's Largest Slave Rebellion and the Man Who Led It, David M. Robertson, Knopf, 1999.
"Denmark Vessey and his Co-Conspirators", Michael Johnson, The William and Mary Quarterly, Oct. 2001.

RODOLFO WALSH
Operación Masacre, Rodolfo Walsh, Planeta, 1998 (in Spanish).
True Crime: Rodolfo Walsh and the Role of the Intellectual in Latin American Politics, Michael McCaughan, Latin America Bureau, 2002.

IDA B. WELLS-BARNETT
Ida: A Sword Among Lions: Ida B. Wells and the Campaign Against Lynching, Paula J. Giddings, Amistad, 2008.
Ida b. Wells-Barnett and American Reform 1880-1930, Patricia A. Schechter, The University of North Carolina Press, 2001.

EMILIANO ZAPATA
Zapata and the Mexican Revolution, John Womack, Vintage, 1970.
Emiliano Zapata!: Revolution and Betrayal in Mexico, Samuel Brunk, University of New Mexico Press, 1995.

ZUMBI DOS PALMARES
Genesis (Memory of Fire, #1), Eduardo Galeano, W. W. Norton & Company, 1998.

JUSTSEEDS ARTISTS' COOPERATIVE {*www.justseeds.org*}
is a decentralized community of artists who have banded together to both sell their work online in a central location and to collaborate with and support each other and social movements.

JESUS BARRAZA is an activist printmaker, artist and techie based in San Leandro, California. Using bold colors and high contrast images his prints reflect both his local and global community and their resistance in a struggle to create a new world. Barraza has worked closely with numerous community organizations creating prints that deal with issues of immigration, homelessness, education, indigeneity, and international solidarity movements.

KEVIN CAPLICKI was born and raised in the Hudson Valley, now living in Brooklyn, NY. He utilizes 3-D installation, stencils, screenprinting, photography, and the ol' pencil & paper to communicate, quite bluntly, anti-imperialist politics and daydreams of utopia.

MELANIE CERVANTES is an Oakland-based Xicana artist activist who views her work as a part of movements for global social justice producing her work in various mediums including pen and ink, acrylic, screenprints, and paper stencils. Employing vibrant colors and hand drawn illustrations her work moves those viewed as marginal to the center and features subjects such as empowered youth, elders, women, queers, indigenous people and communities of color.

ALEC "ICKY" DUNN is an illustrator and printmaker from Portland, OR.

MOLLY FAIR is a Brooklyn, NY-based artist, activist, and soon-to-be librarian. She works in various mediums including screenprinting and video, and is interested in the intersections of art, social justice, and popular education.

NICOLAS LAMPERT is a Milwaukee/Chicago-based interdisciplinary artist who focuses on collage, graphic art, printmaking, research, and curating. His prints address themes of social justice and sustainability and his series "machine-animal collages" speaks about a world engulfed within its own technology.

JOSH MACPHEE is an artist, activist, researcher, curator and author based in Brooklyn, NY. He makes screenprints, often based on themes of radical history and anti-capitalism.

FERNANDO MARTÍ is an artist, community architect, and activist in San Francisco. He is involved in the SF Print Collective. His intent as a printmaker, installation artist and altar-maker is to explore the clash of the Third World in the heart of Empire, and the tension between inhabiting place and the urge to build something transformative.

COLIN MATTHES, based in Milwaukee, WI, works across a range of media including printmaking, drawing, installation, public art, and zine-making. His flat, brusque, obsessive work asks discomfiting questions about our relationships in the world and our participation in activities we do not necessarily endorse.

DYLAN MINER is an artist, theorist, and historian. He produces didactic prints (relief and serigraph) that challenge the ambiguity of the contemporary art world. A diasporic Métis, he migrates between Three Fires Territory (Michigan) and Aztlán (New Mexico). He teaches at Michigan State University.

ROGER PEET lives in Oregon, where he makes prints of various sorts. He spends a lot of time thinking about bugs, fish, birds, mammals, reptiles, amphibians, trilobites, salps, nudibranchs etcetera, and the big red button labeled extinction that keeps being pushed.

JESSE PURCELL is an artist and professional screenprinter living in Montreal, Quebec.

FAVIANNA RODRIGUEZ is an Oakland-based artist-activist, printmaker, technologist and entrepreneur. Named by *UTNE* Magazine as one of the country's leading visionary artists, Rodriguez is renowned for her vibrant posters dealing with social issues such as war, immigration, globalization, and social movements.

{ARTISTS}

ERIK RUIN is a Michigan-raised, Philly-based printmaker, shadow-puppeteer, and occasional editor of various publications, most recently the anthology *Realizing the Impossible: Art Against Authority* (w/ Josh MacPhee, AK Press, 2007). Ongoing theatrical work includes *The Nothing Factory*, an epic musical shadow theater extravaganza, and various improvisational groupings of overhead projectors and musical instruments.

SHAUN SLIFER is a multi-disciplinary artist currently living and gardening in Pittsburgh, PA. His work includes video, letterpress and screenprinting combined with stenciling, kinetic sculpture, and public signage of dubious legality.

CHRIS STAIN is originally from Baltimore and currently lives in Queens, NY. Initially inspired by NYC subway graffiti, Chris' stencil work and screen prints revolve around his inner city working class upbringing. With his work he hopes to inspire compassion and understanding for less fortunate members of society.

MEREDITH STERN lives in the woods in Providence, RI, hunting mushrooms, banging drums, and cutting linoleum block prints.

MARY TREMONTE is an artist-educator-DJ living in Pittsburgh, PA, consumed with printmaking, totally teens, communication, and the politics of social space, particularly the dance party. Her silkscreen prints often use animals to explore complex themes, such as queerness and the possibility for change.

KRISTINE VIRSIS is a printmaker living and working in NYC. She produces silkscreen prints, which begin as intricate paper cuts and stencils, dealing with the personal end of the political spectrum—creativity, self-sufficiency, nostalgia, as well as mental health and resiliency.

PETE YAHNKE was raised in the north-woods of Wisconsin, taught himself printmaking and now spends his time carving large pieces of linoleum into images.

BEC YOUNG is a Detroit-rooted, Pittsburgh-based artist who seeks to inspire—and draw inspiration from—movements for social justice.

{INDEX}